THE FUN BOOK OF
FATHERHOOD

A Paternity Leave Dad—Tale of a Pioneer

With his children,
They Explore the Secrets of the Wild Kingdom

Jerry Cammarata

with
Frances Spatz Leighton

Corwin Books – Los Angeles – 1st Edition
Christian Faith Publishing– 2nd Edition

ISBN 978-1-64140-611-6 (paperback)
ISBN 978-1-64140-613-0 (hardcover)
ISBN 978-1-64140-612-3 (digital)

Christian Faith Publishing, Inc.
832 Park Avenue
Meadville, PA 16335
www.christianfaithpublishing.com

Originally Presented in cooperation with Lou Reda Productions and Stan Corwin Publishing

Printed in the United States of America

Penny Stoil
Editor

The animals in this book along with my family were wonderfully served by the very competent and sensitive editing of Penny Stoil. The role of an editor is often not appreciated as well as it should. The creative energy of any author becomes even more successful in telling a story when an editor's keen eye for style is applied. Much like a chameleon, Penny was able to live alongside the animal experiences and the daily activities of the family and, while becoming them, edit the book into a beautiful series of learning vignettes for all to enjoy for years and years to come.

This book is respectfully dedicated to the
great unsung animal parents of the world.

Dedication

To my wife, Margy, the lioness, without who I wouldn't have had 'em to write about. Truly, the matriarch of our human animal kingdom at home who nurtured and unselfishly gave her energy and wisdom to our three beautiful children. Her example of family is the high bar of perfection.

To our daughters, Elizabeth and Michelle, the beavers, kittens, and monkeys in my life, who have showed me definitively that no two things are alike.

To our son, Jerry, who was born after the original book was written, however, is the squirrel of the family—an expert in making sure we save for a rainy day. It was a delight to see the nurturing given to Jerry by his oldest sisters and even greater delight to see Jerry grow into an outstanding parent himself.

To our newest baby cubs—granddaughters and grandson—Anna 8; Julia 6; Alessandra 5; Anthony 2; our family awaits the day when you clear the nest and your future is all you wish it to be.

"I feel like a rhino rushing through the forest—I have no idea where I'm going until I get the scent and, *zingo*, then I know where I'm going and what to do."

"All parents are a little like rhinos—absolutely at a loss. So, read and relax. In the raising of kids, I always say it's good to know whatever we try, somewhere in the animal kingdom, someone else has tried it first!"

Contents

Acknowledgments

To my co-author, Frances Spatz Leighton, who wins the animal kingdom award of being the nicest animal.

To Congressman Gary Ackerman for his legislative wisdom in furthering paternity leave back in the 70s.

To Sister Agnes, former principal of St Sylvester's School, who, when I was in the third grade, made me pray in front of the Blessed Mother Statue for changing all the 50's on my report card to 100's so my parents would not be mad at me.

To the members of the news media, especially Dr. Jeffrey Gardere, who have supported my commitment to a national policy on parenting leave.

To my parents, Mary and Jerry, who never denied me anything and who always insisted that what I received I wouldn't abuse but use to the best of my ability. Specifically to my mother, who never let us out of her house without eating and giving the kids a toy. To my father, who knew he had a son who couldn't do plumbing, electrical work, or carpentry as well as he could, and who was always there when Michelle put the towel down the toilet bowl and Elizabeth managed to run over the electric cord with the lawn mower.

To my mother-in-law, Ida, and father-in-law, Jim, who were the first to know of my brainy ideas, and who had to live with me. A house without them would have truly made for a lesser life.

To Jacques Cousteau, who never knew it but was constantly being watched and studied in our living room on television.

To the animal kingdom for supplying me with all I needed to know about how to be a daddy, and then some. *You* are always welcome over our house.

To Lisa and her father, the late Oscar Collier, who, like greyhounds, raced to get the first edition of the book published, and who have remained friends for all these decades.

To my first publisher Stan Corwin, who viewed my book, not as a story to be told, but rather as a concerned parent himself who was interested in making parenting more enjoyable and interesting to more people. His commitment to the family structure and confidence in me produced the underlying motivation for the construction of the first edition of this book and his influence on this edition.

To Lou Reda, Max Rosey, and Morty Matz, who, like the busiest and most creative of animals, have given an enormous amount of assistance in making this book possible.

To my literary consultant, Jerry Schmitterer, who clawed his way through the density of the manuscript, and offered invaluable assistance.

To Dr. Jerry Ross for his encouragement to write this book and his enthusiasm for always keeping education at the center of conversation.

To Steve Aiello, *the ultimate beaver.* Like a beaver, he helped build the great lodge called the NYC Board of Education and honored the role moms and dads should and must play in education. Steve is an unsung hero of our modern education system.

To Brian Laline, the longtime editor of the Staten Island Advance, I am grateful to you and your writers for embracing so many stories about education, family, social justice, and political responsibility. You have played an important role in moving the agenda of family equity locally and nationally.

A Special Acknowledgement:

To all the women who have done so much, directly and indirectly, to support equality in the home, at work, in politics, in education, and in all we are. Thanks to Gloria Steinem, Eleanor Pam, Muriel Fox, Congresswoman Shirley Chisholm, Congresswoman Bella Abzug, and Dr. Marian Diamond and so many others.

Prologue

When I first sat down to write this book in 1974, I was fresh from the emboldening experience of being the first male teacher in the history of New York City Board of Education (if not the country) to be granted a paternity leave. I was the first to be able to enjoy the wonders of my children at the most formative time of their lives, without putting my family livelihood and career at risk. I knew then this was the right thing to do, and I would not be the last to do it.

Providing some necessary and validating discussion on FAMILY LEAVE, before we enter the world of my experiences as a dad at home with mom and the kids, it is important to reflect on what our future commitment to parenting must be.

Today, it is commonplace around the world (not so much the United States, unfortunately) for men to take paid family leave to be with their wives and children at an irreplaceable time in their lives.

Thinking back, it is hard to imagine how little support my quest for paternity leave garnered, even from my own family. They thought I was crazy! "Are you going to wear an apron around the house?" was a typical taunt. The expression "Mr. Mom" wasn't part of the vernacular then, but the thought was. Friends, family, and co-workers just could not understand it.

While great strides have been made in our approach to family leave in the United States, we still have a long and winding path to travel. According to a 2016 study by Pew Research Center, in almost 50% of two parent households in the United States, both parents work, and in 40% of all families the mother is the primary or sole breadwinner. A study of 41 countries indicates that the United States is the only country that does not provide for paid family leave. Of these 41 nations, the shortest time allowed is two months and the longest is two years. While it is true that paid leave is predominantly directed towards mothers, 31 of these countries also provide this benefit to fathers.

Japan is the most generous country offering fathers up to 30 weeks (although on average fathers generally receive two weeks). In fairness, it should be emphasized that although the U.S. doesn't yet have a national policy on family leave, a growing number of states and business do provide this benefit. However, given the importance of developing parental bonds and a positive and nurturing environment for newborns, my position has always been that the cost of not providing family leave outweighs allowing for it. Some things cannot be measured in dollars and cents.

In 2016, I looked on with pride as the U.S. made great progress towards protecting our families. New York State passed the nation's strongest paid family leave program to date, California expanded their decade-old law to increase the wage replacement rates, and the city of San Francisco passed a paid parental leave ordinance. These laws built on existing paid family leave legislation in Rhode Island, New Jersey and California, as well as the 1993 federal Family and Medical Leave Act (FMLA), which grants certain employees unpaid leave with job protection. However, the vast majority of Americans are still left with no choice but dependency on their employer's discretion of what fair leave policies are.

In 2016, Secretary of Labor Tom Perez was moved to say; "If you have to choose between the family that you love and the job that you need, that's a really unfair choice. That is what's happening all across America."

Perez said that women are returning to work far sooner than what is healthy for them and their babies.

The health benefits for children, whose parents, mothers and fathers are able to be with them during the earliest formative days of their lives, are undisputed. That's what my instinct told me in 1972 when I attempted to sue the New York City Board of Education for the honor to become the first male parent to be granted paternity leave. The board had no choice but to grant me the paternity leave after an incredible action taken by the Federal Employment Opportunities Commission in this regard. It all fit into place.

But, my groundbreaking leave from the country's largest school district left me adrift without a life raft; this leave was unpaid. Being ahead of the times, there were no HR policies on paternity leaves, no cultural awareness for community support, and no financial programs to support this radical idea. Today, that situation has improved dramatically, but there is still so much work to be done.

Corporate America, especially the Silicon Valley companies, are leading the way in ensuring that every employee has the opportunity to raise their children in a progressive manner that has proven beneficial all over the world. And I point out in this book, we still have a lot to learn from the animal kingdom. The time has arrived. Hi-tech companies, including Twitter, Facebook, Netflix and Microsoft, have joined the movement, and governments from Albany to Sacramento are making it law. Even companies that go back generations, like Coca-Cola, are on board. But, the list must grow.

Unfortunately in the United States, women still fear that taking time off to raise their babies will have a negative effect on their careers. It is hard to argue with that. In the workplace no matter how progressive the employer, maternity leave still carries a stigma. Bosses do not like losing the services of key personnel for any reason. It is even worse for men.

And, family leave is still too often an unpaid benefit putting too much pressure on the father or mother. Today's families are commonly led by two working parents, whose children are put in day care or pre-school. Heck, we're talking pre-toilet training in order for both salaries to resume as quickly as possible.

We are a work-oriented society and that ethic has done well for us over the last three centuries. We were a social experiment in 1776, and have never stopped experimenting. We talk a lot about family values. What is more valuable than paid family leave in an atmosphere of understanding that enables a career to continue to blossom? I do not think we lose anything by gaining more valuable time with our infant children.

In many countries the gap between the "haves" and "have nots" continue to grow, and there is an increasing sense of inequality across America and other developed nations. What better time is there to remind people that social change can advance through the actions of one father who realized that spending time with his children would give them a chance to achieve the success that they and all our children deserve?

Who can we proclaim as the heroes of parenting? Do we discount our forefathers in establishing our great constitution? Do we embrace the women who fought for suffrage and equal rights for women? Do we congratulate the scientists and physicians who provided empirical evidence in raising children, and do we point to ourselves proudly as a contributor of good parenting standards? May all of these constituencies enter a Hall of Family Practice, and take the place at the table. It will take all of us to get to this point.

And now, what it was like to be that parent, enjoying and loving every minute of being on paternity leave.

CHAPTER 1

The Animals of the Zoo Are Alive and Well and Helping to Raise the Kids at Our House

Little Liz, age eight, wants to furnish hot water bottles to kangaroos—the babies may get cold in that pouch. Michelle wants to turn an airplane into Noah's ark, march the animals in, two by two, which, incidentally, is just half her own age of four. I may as well confess; this is not your average household.

Me? I'm raising our brood by the rules of the animal kingdom. And if you are wondering how I have time for such goings-on, let me tell you that I'm the first man in history to go on paternity leave. No, I didn't have the babies. My wife, Margy, did. She's the only sane one in our house, or at least she was until I came up with this idea when she was pregnant with our second child.

I said, "Margy, you've had one baby. Let's do something different. Let's rethink parenthood. Let's see what the animals do."

Margaret looked at me coldly. "Do they know something we don't know? What about Dr. Spock and the other books you pushed on me? What are you trying to say?" asked Margy.

"I'm saying let's take a look at the animal kingdom to see how the creatures of the world handle the problems of parenting. Wait till you see my new bag of tricks along other lines," I leered at her. "Masters and Johnson should consult the otter."

"Okay," said Margy, "here we go again. I'll try your new scheme, but what will we do with all these baby books?"

"I'll think of something," I said.

Fatherhood! Motherhood! A whole lot of grimly serious books have been written about the state-of-the-art. This isn't one of them. In fact, if you want to moan and groan about the problems of parenthood, skip this book. But if you want to relax and enjoy parenting and you want a glimpse of what various animals do, come with me into the animal kingdom. As a bonus, you will have the comfort of realizing you're not the only critter who has problems in raising the young. You are not alone. Whatever you can think of, some animal did it first. Nor am I saying that every animal is a great parent. There are good fathers, and there are fathers who would eat their young if the mothers let down their guard.

There are good mothers and then there is the cuckoo. The cuckoo, or cowbird as she is called in the United States, is about as selfish a mother as you can find. She refuses to waste her time raising her young, or even to hustle around long enough to make a nest for her eggs. Instead, she sneakily deposits her eggs in someone else's nest, even if her egg is larger and very obviously a ringer. But the gentle bird in whose nest the egg was deposited generously accepts the egg and then amazingly hatches it along with her own.

At first, the baby cowbird acts like all the other birds, opening wide to receive all the worms and bugs it can get. But, proving that a bad egg is always a bad egg, the little cuckoo-cowbird immediately pushes the rightful progeny out of the nest and takes all the food itself. The poor mama and papa birds find they have raised a monster. They cannot haul their own offspring back up into the nest, and they are therefore stuck with the imposter. And yet, such is the instinct of parenthood that they keep right on slavishly bringing food to it until it flies away.

Once Margy, little Liz, and I were witnessed a starling as it took over a flicker's nest in a half-rotten branch. The lady flicker was in there with her bill protruding, and the starling was sitting up above her on a nearby branch watching, waiting for her chance. When the flicker left for a moment, probably to get some food, the starling darted in and took over.

Eventually, the flicker gave up and supposedly found other quarters. But, there is poetic justice. It came to pass one stormy day that the whole limb and nest fell down, and Madam Starling got her come uppance. You get it? Nature handled it her own way.

* * *

Forget Spock.

Forget Dodson; ditto, Ginott.

Forget Gersh and all the rest of those child experts, at least for a while.

The more you read their advice, their prepackaged rhetoric, the more uptight you get. The only real experts on parenting are the animals of the world. Left in the wild, they can really show you how to handle your own children without getting unnerved at every new development.

Don't think you're unique. Almost any problem you have, the animals have faced too.

At our house, the kids found better use for the great books of child experts by using them to provide elevation at the kitchen table, or a substitute for a door stop, or a window prop. So much for the experts. We'll give them a little credit later. But for now, let's listen to the animals.

First, to set the stage. Parents are divided into multiple categories.

Those in which the animal mother raises the offspring unaided by her mate.

Those in which the animal father raises the kids alone.

Those in which the animal babies it together.

Those in which the animal kids do it themselves, saying, in effect, "We don't need anybody and nuts to both of you."

And what are the human species divided into?

Those in which the divorced father is raising the kids and the mother feels guilty.

Those in which the divorced mother is raising the kids and the father feels guilty.

Those in which the mother and father are raising the kids together and they both feel guilty.

Those in which the grandparents or grandparents must raise the kids and everybody feels guilty.

Those in which the kids are raising themselves and society feels guilty.

What do the animals know that we don't know? They know that not everybody is meant to be a parent. They just do what comes naturally. Ergo, no guilt.

For some reason, the human race thinks that a mother must act like a mother. Sometimes fathers make the best mothers.

I say we have to look around, relax, enjoy parenthood, and not be so concerned about the storybook ideal home with Mother at its helm. Let's try doing what comes naturally. Then because we are relaxed, maybe we can raise children who are relaxed too, lessening the chance that they will get into major trouble in their young lives.

Do you see animals turning into criminals? Hell, no! A rogue elephant is a rare thing. An animal that goes around killing for the hell of it is a rare thing. But a kid in juvenile court is an everyday thing. In fact, we are now at the point where too many juveniles are committing crimes and going to jail.

As I have said before, not every mother is meant to be a parent, and the courts prove it in child abuse cases every day. Even the animals of nature recognize this. The African honeyguide bird would die rather than take care of her young. Like the cuckoo, she drops her egg in someone else's nest and is done with it. Let someone else raise the kid.

Fella, you think you know about female irresponsibility?

Nature abounds in female creatures wriggling their way out of responsibility. Think of the poor male phalarope, a decent sort of water fowl doomed from the start. Once a particular female has set her sights on him, she makes life an unmitigated hell until he surrenders.

She flaunts herself before him on the water and demands his attention. If he ignores her, she screams at him, jumps about, and then tries to show how pretty she is by performing a vulgar dance.

She's usually bigger than he is, and, if he is still not captivated by this clumsy bit of demonstration, she bites at him and drives him out of the water to her nest.

What can he do? He lets her have her way with him and finally mates with her. And what does she do? She lets him think it is forever. But as soon as her eggs are fertilized and safely in the nest, she takes off, deserts him, leaves him flat. Old phalarope is left in complete charge of the household while she runs around with her equally peculiar sisters having a good time, screaming with laughter, and acting as if she didn't have a responsibility in the world, which, believe me, she doesn't.

My situation is not quite like that. I opted to play fatherhood big. People do a double take when they learn that I am on paternity leave. Actually, I should be the one looking askance at them because of how little the average human male participates in this great adventure in which he played such a major role in bringing it about.

Some animals, and even some species of insects, take a much greater interest in paternity. In some ways, fathering is becoming a dying art. In years gone by, certain societies practiced something called couvade, which I understand may still be a part of the culture in Latin countries.

It's a switching of roles as soon as the baby is born. The mother gets out of bed and gets back into her normal housework routine, and the father gets into her bed and stays there with the baby. There are two theories on this. One is that the father is jealous of all the attention the mother and newborn are given and wants to get in on it. The other is that he is taking precautionary steps to prevent the great letdown feeling some women experience after childbirth. They've done it, and it's over.

They've waited nine months, and now the baby is here, and somehow it isn't all it was cracked up to be. It's amazing how humans have sometimes taken a leaf from the animals. Some believe that the practice of couvade was originated by the Chinese after seeing how birds and waterfowl shared in the burden of sitting on and watching over the eggs through to childbirth, and then constantly feeding the young birds.

But can you imagine the havoc it would cause if fathers burst into the hospital maternity wards and insisted that their wives get out of bed and they get in. In my case, I was too late to get in on couvade. My paternity leave, which I had applied for early in Margy's pregnancy, did not come through until Michelle had been in this big wide world for four months.

I do not know the entire implication of our animalistic approach to parenting, but I certainly hope sociologists will study it further. Meanwhile, I'm having a great time being a parent and feeling sorry for my friends who are still approaching the parenting experience in a stereotypical way.

An additional benefit is that I believe my kids have already learned to respect all the inhabitants of the world, not just their own kind. I am sure you will never find my daughters dressed in the fur of wild animals. It would be like killing a friend. But this is my own supposition. At this writing, Liz has announced that she will not even wear a sheepskin coat because she would be embarrassed if seen by another sheep.

*   *   *

Children are simply fascinated to learn how creatures other than themselves do things, or perform in some unusual way. The kids of the neighborhood have waited in the yard for many hours with Michelle, Liz, and me in the hopes that a hummingbird would show up so that we could see how fast those wings could flutter—sixty times a second, 4200 times a minute.

All of them were entranced to learn that grasshoppers do not have ears where little children have ears. Baby grasshoppers and their daddies and mommies have ears in their front legs. So do katydids.

*   *   *

Our backyard is a wildlife sanctuary. Any bird or bug, stray cat or dog is welcome. So are the roses, the irises, the chrysanthemums.

I thought we had everything back there, but Elizabeth pointed out that butterflies were missing. She was not happy about it.

There were lots of butterflies up the street in a very messy yard, but our yard was so pretty, we certainly deserved to have butterflies too. On that we both agreed. But wishing doesn't make it so, as I frequently pointed out to Liz, "So, as people of action, let's get things done."

"Okay," said Liz, used to our routine by now, "call an expert."

"Who's an expert on butterflies?" I wondered aloud.

"Call the zoo," Liz suggested. The Staten Island Zoo is always her first thought, and the Bronx Zoo her next.

"I don't think zoos have butterflies," I said, "but we can always try a university entomology department or an agricultural department."

By luck, we found someone at the Staten Island Zoo on the first call. He knew how to entice butterflies to his own backyard. "It's easy," he said. "All you have to do is provide an area in your yard where you let weeds and grass just grow. Butterflies do not like neat lawns. We have a butterfly corner in our yard, with a border of roses in front of it, so that it doesn't look too bad. To be sure that butterflies do come, we've planted butterfly bushes that can be ordered from a nursery. The technical name is Buddleia."

The zoo man mentioned several other plants that attract butterflies that could be planted in a butterfly corner such as petunias, asters, black-eyed Susans, and butterfly weed, a milkweed that blossoms into bright orange flowers. It can be ordered by its proper name, *Asclepias tuberosa*.

*   *   *

When we face a new problem at our house, we are apt to sit around and talk about what the various animals of the world would do about it. I'm remembering a very important time when Elizabeth was playing in the hot summer sun and would not slow down.

Finally, the heat and excitement got the best of her, and we had a sick little girl on our hands. After we had wrapped her up and fed her liquids and nursed her back to health, we had a family meeting, inviting in some animals. The whole zoo was there in our imagination, putting in their sage bits of advice.

The jungle lion said it was silly to run around in the hot sun when you could find a nice, cool, shady spot under a tree and watch everyone else run around. "Stay cool, man," said Jerry Lion.

The bat said the children had no reason whatever to be outside in such heat and ought to be curled up inside the house hanging from the ceiling. Squeaked the bat over my shoulder, "You people are all upside down!"

The otter said that it was alright for the to be outside, but Liz should have been lying on her back in the pool. "Happiness is rocking in the water with an abalone on your tummy." That was the voice of Margy Otter.

The beaver said that at her house on Beaver Island, she had the same problem of exhaustion and suggested that as Elizabeth should just ignore it. "Hup, two, three, four. Hup, two, three, four." A beaver never gives up, just keeps rushing around dragging wood, getting it into the water, and adding to the beaver dam as if the safety of the whole world depended on it. "And it really does, you know. Ask any beaver."

Liz giggled. A good sign, a good sign, indeed.

"What did Elizabeth think about it?" Margy and I asked. "Did she want to be like a beaver who would never quit and just keeps working until she gets exhausted?"

No, Elizabeth didn't want to be a beaver.

"Did she want to be an otter and lie on her back in our backyard plastic pool?"

No, she didn't want to get all wet and not be able to wear a pretty dress.

"Did she want to hang upside down from the ceiling like a bat?"

"No, you can't fool me," said Elizabeth. "I know that heat rises."

"Well, Elizabeth," I said, "shall we look around the jungle some more, or would you just like to be the lion?"

"Yes," said Liz, pleased at last to see a connection that suited her. "Can I take my new book outside and sit under the tree with a pillow like the lion?"

"The male lion, Liz," I said. "Just pretend you're a male lion. The lioness is probably off somewhere stalking food. And a little lion like you would probably be right behind her on her first lion hunt."

I'm teaching my kids they can't escape conformity altogether, but only to a reasonable extent. I'm telling them that they are lucky to be people, because at the very least they can show some individuality without punishment. In animal societies, the one who doesn't conform may get thrown out of the group immediately and stand a good chance of starving, or being ripped off by the first gang of predators that comes along.

Those animals who merely get thrown out of the community are lucky. In some animal societies, like a flock of chickens, say, the other chickens simply peck it to death.

Elizabeth was amazed to hear that some chickens consider themselves better than other chickens. "Well, honey, they certainly do," I told her. "As you grow up you will hear a lot about the 'pecking order.' That got its name from the chickens who think they are such hot shots that they have the right to peck a chicken who is not so important or so popular."

"That sounds like my class at school," said Liz. "There's a girl who thinks she's so smart and she's mean to this other girl."

"Right on, honeychild," I said. "That's it, exactly. And the way it works in the henyard is this: a new flock of chickens is put in there. The first few days some of them will seem to mind their own business, while others are very nasty and fight every time they meet, taking a peck at each other's head or flying at each other in a rage with wings flapping. They are establishing the pecking order."

"What do you mean?" asked Liz.

"One backs down, and from then on the victor has the right to peck that chicken whenever it feels like it. The boss of the flock is the chicken who can peck any chicken she wants. She's not afraid of anybody."

"But what happens to the nice little chickens who just minded their own business?" Liz wanted to know.

"Well, since they won't fight, almost anyone can peck them. The chickens in the yard eventually have a whole complicated order of who can peck whom. There is a number two chicken, and she can peck anyone but the top boss. And then there are chickens who can peck other chickens who are not as good as they are, all the way down the ladder."

"I don't like it," said Elizabeth. "I don't like that story."

"But it's true," I assured her. "It's a fact of life, and what you can learn from it is that you are lucky to be a human and not have to physically fight everyone you see in order to reach the top. You can do it by being good at something you do—like in school, or in sports, or in writing or using your imagination some way."

She was much relieved.

"But there is another lesson I want you to learn from the chicken," I said. "You know, some people have a little mean streak, just like some animals do."

"I know," she said. "That girl at school has a real mean streak."

"Well, if a chicken gets a little wound on its head and there is a little blood showing or just bare skin, that puts the chicken way down the social ladder. All the other chickens think they have the right to peck it some more. And you know, sometimes they hurt that poor chicken badly before the farmer notices and takes that chicken out to save its life."

"Well, I don't know what that has to do with me. Even the mean girl doesn't hit the other girl that hard."

"No, I don't mean necessarily physical hitting. I also mean people who are nasty and say unkind things at school, even later when you grow up. What I'm trying to say, dear, is that if you act wounded all the time, the ones who are a little mean and think they are better than anyone else will start pecking at you more, not with their bills, like a chicken, but with unkind words that can hurt just as much."

"Oh, yes, she does that."

"Well, if you are the target of that kind of mean talk, don't act wounded. Just act haughty, as if you couldn't care less, or tell her you don't care what she thinks. And don't bother to try to please her, she's just a mean chicken."

"I won't try. This other girl gives her candy and things, and she's still cruel to her."

"You see what I mean?"

I hope Liz does. The lesson of the chicken is one of the most important ones that a child can learn in order to protect its pride and stay out of trouble. If mankind followed the lifestyle of the chicken, the roughest, toughest human would be permitted to walk in first, grab the food he wanted before anybody else got any, choose his bed first, throw out anyone he didn't want around him, and pick any sexual partner who struck his fancy at any particular moment, whether anyone liked it or not. All would act submissively and be humble around him. No male or female would dare refuse him.

Come to think of it, we do have that in some places in the world, and it's called a dictatorship!

CHAPTER 2

Daddy's Home on Paternity Leave

In the beginning was the word, and the word was paternity leave.

When people ask me how I happened to come up with the crazy idea of demanding and fighting for paternity leave, I say the ancient books made me do it although a little late in my marriage.

It might seem that paternity leave is supposed to see the husband through the birth of his first child. I lost out on that because baby Elizabeth was already here, but I saw the light of understanding when wife Margaret was very pregnant with our second child. Of course nobody took me seriously at first, including my wife. When she realized I really was going to fight for paternity leave, she was somewhat indignant.

So were my in-laws, who called a clan meeting at my house to decide what to do about this nut who had married into the family. Though I was an only child, my wife had many relatives within a half-hour radius, and all who could come came, and sat in a solemn circle, tsk-tsking and shaking their heads. Snatches of conversation filtered through to me. Joseph, Margaret's draftsman brother, labeled paternity leave "unnatural and foolish" "only the mother is responsible for the rearing of the child certainly during the first year."

Nick, Margaret's fireman brother, groaned at having his fireman buddies know about his brother in-law's "totally crazy venture into fatherhood. Maybe we should take him to a shrink."

I was not exactly a part of this meeting. In fact, I had been treated like the invisible man as all the big cars rolled up and the successful relatives climbed out, greeting Margaret as if there had been a death in the family and I was the departed loved one.

As the discussion got to "what will become of our Margaret and her babies and how will he support the house," I jumped into the conversation to announce, "I'm selling the house and buying a bigger one so that you folks can live in it too." I pointed a finger at my father-in-law, Jim Pucciarelli.

"What? What?" he shouted.

As a gasp echoed around the room, I tried to smile with confidence. Frankly, it was the first time I had sprung that idea on them. In fact, this solution had just popped into my own mind. But then that's what education is all about. I had been training for years to come up with new solutions. I was used to switching boats in midstream; even used to swimming upstream against the tide. And yes, I was used to family compromises, a very touchy business. But this was certainly an abrupt switch for me, even considering that I had veered away from my mother's wish for me to be a banker. Actually, my burning desire had been to go into the theater because I felt I had a natural flair. My mother's burning desire was for me to have steady work.

I didn't plan to be a Robert Redford, and I was pretty far short of being a six-footer like Cary Grant, but I saw myself as another Dustin Hoffman, or better yet, Woody Allen. My father offered a compromise. If I went to college and stuck with it, I could major in anything I wanted, even acting. Somewhere in the halls of ivy, he was sure I would have to take at least one course that would earn me a job if the theater did not pan out.

My grades in high school had been good enough to get me into a special program at Hofstra University. It was called New College, a stepped-up program that enabled me to have a bachelor's degree in three years instead of four. In my last year, I needed a job on campus to help with car expenses and odds and ends. I went to my department chairman, Dr. Jack Tureen, who later became chairman of the Speech Science Department at Hofstra. I asked him for a job within the department. He said all he had was a part-time job in the speech clinic and sent me to have a look. When I saw through a one-way mirror little children struggling to learn to speak normally in order to overcome various handicaps, I felt a great upheaval within me. I had found my cause.

Theater was not the only thing now of value in life. Before I knew it, I had loaded my schedule of course work with enough subjects to also earn a degree in speech language pathology and audiology. I was learning that the greatest thrill in life was not to make people laugh, but to help the less fortunate. It was a great feeling. I went on to take masters and doctorate work in the subject. Stuttering, physical deformities, poor hearing, and various psychogenic deficiencies causing speech problems had me hooked. I had found someone who needed me—the little children. I could clown with them and help them have fun while straightening out their speech difficulties. Theater plus.

I taught three years in the New York City Public School System, specializing in speech therapy. I also had a part-time consultancy at a public health hospital. That added a few more dollars to my earnings. To add still more, I had a few private patients and entertained some evenings with a little band I put together.

Everything was fine, except that I was missing out on the most important experience of all, my own role as a father. I hardly knew my little daughter, and when Elizabeth was three, Margy was again pregnant.

At that time, I was talking so much about the rat race that I was in, that Elizabeth asked me one day as I was leaving for work to bring her home a rat!

"A rat?" I yelled, as I turned back to look at her. "Where would I get a rat?"

"From the rat race, Daddy," she screamed back.

Surely I had to get acquainted with my own child. It was at that psychological moment that I read something that changed my life. It was that the New York State Higher Board of Education was proposing that New York State college professors be allowed time off to help their wives take care of their children. This was it! Paternity leave! No such thing had ever been granted, and I was determined to be the frontrunner. It wasn't hard to do. The field was wide open. Fathers were not flocking to apply for baby care duty, and the press was amused.

But I was not. I was dead serious. As I stated in an open letter to the press: "As paternity leave becomes a reality, the isolated nuclear family as we know it today in the United States will take on another dimension, if not completely change. I believe that the change is good and long needed."

"Our family structure is becoming too sterile, mechanical, and adult-oriented, and is not devoted to the total development of the children as it should be. The formative years of our children cannot be wasted due to economic conditions that force parents away from their loved ones."

A whole nation got involved in my fight, and newspaper columnists wrote articles and editorials about one Jerry Cammarata who had fought city hall and come away with a four-year paternity leave (although without pay) the first man to get it."

During the four years of my leave, about the cutest letter I got from all the thousands I received came from Kathy Gangwisch, a public relations person in Los Angeles. She wrote:

> "Congratulations to you personally for taking such an interest in your children; I think it's worth a hundred stars on your toothbrush chart, as they used to tell me in kindergarten!"

*   *   *

It is important to note that Congressman Gary Ackerman was very instrumental in working toward making paternity leave a reality for men. Because of his efforts on the congressional level, the Federal Equal Employment Opportunities Commission agreed to include equal time off for dads. This decision by the FEEOC was key to the New York City Board of Education granting me the first Paternity Leave.

My voice, my concern, and my passion for what I believed in was heard in the 70s by the President of the New York City Central Board of Education, Dr. Steve Aiello. Dr. Aiello convened a meeting of the entire Central Board and secured a unanimous decision to grant me the first ever paternity Leave. According to Dr. Aiello, "The richness of education is to acknowledge changing times and to understand how those changing times can have an impact on children. Jerry became the beacon of hope for dads throughout the country, if not the world, to reassess their commitment to their families, and to begin to feel empowered to share in the parenting responsibilities of their children. Because of Jerry's bold action, families today can decide on what is good for them and not always guided by what corporate America wants. Jerry's journey down the path of parenting and being granted a paternity leave, was one of the most profound decisions made by me and unanimously by the members of the New York City Central Board of Education." Interestingly, I am still very good friends with Steve today.

Some 30 years later, continuing my activist role on the local, state and national level, promoting paternity leave, I was appointed a member to the same New York City Central Board of Education which granted me that historic landmark decision. From 1995 to 2002, I was responsible now for 1.1 million students, 1100 school buildings, approximately 100,000 teachers and staff, and an educational budget of #13 billion. The only one in New York City government, Mayor Rudy Giuliani concurrently appointed me to be the Commissioner of the New York City Department of Youth and Community Development, where I operated a budget of $155 million, with a staff of 500, and provide programs of literacy, citizenship and after school programs to children and adults throughout the 5 boroughs of New York City.

* * *

When I finally got my paternity leave, baby Michelle, over whom the battle had been fought, was four months old.

Until my wife gave birth, I had been sure it was a false pregnancy. She never craved anything extraordinary. After nine months of not being sent out in the middle of the night for a banana sandwich or a pistachio ice-cream soda, my wife gave birth to a girl.

I admit, I was hoping for a boy this time. But looking back, I must have been out of my mind. Two girls are the ideal family, and when I need a boy, I can always borrow a nephew or even a local Boy Scout troop. As a matter of fact, the word quickly got around that "Super Pop" spent his time at home and in no time I was surrounded by a flock of children clamoring for attention, affection, and solutions to problems. I was Father Goose, Mother Hen, and the Cookie Monster all rolled into one.

*   *   *

Paternity leave meant really cutting costs. No avoidable extra expenses were allowed. No pets. Still I more than made up for it in taking Elizabeth and Michelle, as soon to the zoo. We also found huge posters of animals to tape all over the house.

Furthermore, the pets in the neighborhood were shared equally by Elizabeth and her little friends. She liked a cat named Esmeralda, a white beauty who took up residence at our house whenever the table scraps appealed to her, and especially a small dog named Chuckie.

One day Chuckie and Elizabeth were roaring around the house when I heard a *yip yip*, as if Chuckie was in pain, but it was Lizzie who was letting out a cry of anguish. Finally, I yelled, "Stop it!" and ordered Liz to tell me what was going on. "What kind of game are you playing, anyway?"

"That's all right, Daddy, I'm playing dog." "How do you play dog?" I asked, somewhat pleased that our Saturday animal games were having a carryover effect into real life.

"Oh, it's easy. I chase Chuckie till I find him, then I bite him and try to get away before he bites me back."

Margaret looked at me and shook her head. "I knew you were going too far," she said, shooing the dog out and taking her daughter to the bathroom for a little medicinal touchup job on the red spots.

The cat was a quieter creature, and the only trouble came when Esmeralda got bored and was ready to go home. Liz didn't want her to leave. Unfortunately, the cat always got bored first. One day I came upon Liz clutching the cat by its tail. The cat was being patient and not scratching, but it looked like that was going to be the next step if Liz didn't let go.

"Stop pulling the cat's tail," I said. "Stop!" I said again, angrily. "A cat's tail is not for pulling."

She let go. But she was angry too. "You're mean," she told me. "Daddy, I wasn't pulling the cat's tail." The cat streaked out the door. Liz was crying.

It was time for a little heart-to-heart about honesty, and I picked up Liz and put her on my lap.

"Now, Elizabeth," I said, remembering all of what I had learned from the great experts on child rearing. "I know you are angry and upset that the cat ran home and didn't want to stay with you any longer. But you can't pull a cat's tail."

"I told you, Daddy, I didn't pull the cat's tail. I was just holding it, and the cat pulled its own tail!"

* * *

Meanwhile, life was changing in other ways.

"Are you sure this is a good thing," asked Margaret, "having relatives living with us?"

"It is," I assured her. "It's an extended family. That's the best kind. A little of everything, especially grandparents. They can be assistant parents when you are away. Our children will know all about youth and age and will see a lifespan that the modern child doesn't know anything about. They will respect the elderly. They will know so much love that they will not feel hostility."

By now Grandma lived in our house. So did Grandpa. Instead of moving in with them, they had moved in with us. They decorated the top floor their way, conservative. I was left with the job of decorating the ground and first floor my way. That meant, of course, that most animals of the jungle would feel right at home in our living quarters. A jagged (fake) stone wall covered a large area of the living room, and it was filled with hanging, standing, and sitting plants— comfort for the animals.

When Elizabeth said she didn't want to be the only one among her playmates who has a "granny" at home and asked, "Who else does it, Daddy?" I started my animal game. I rushed to the nearest library and got all kinds of animal picture books that showed extended families of the animal kingdom. One showed how the mountain sheep get in a group, and all the lady sheep stick together and help take care of the young.

But more important to Elizabeth was learning about the elephant's "auntie system."

"The way it works," I explained to little Liz, "is that the expectant mommy, you know, the mommy who's expecting a baby."

"I know. Go on, Daddy."

"The expectant mama elephant seeks out the company of another lady elephant who is older and wiser than she, and they call her the auntie."

"What does she do?"

"Well, Elizabeth, she and the elephant mama come to be good friends, and when the baby is born, the mommy and she stick together to protect the newborn, which is always grazing—one adult elephant walking on each side of the calf. This is to protect the baby from a tiger attack." "Liz, it's like when you walk between mommy and me, we protect you from the moving cars. They are the modern tigers."

"Why doesn't the daddy elephant protect his baby?" Liz was not to be sidetracked. Such a question deserves an answer, and Lizzie has learned that human babies and some animal babies are lucky to have helpful daddies. But some animal daddies are very dangerous, and so only the mother looks after the little ones. Hyena daddies eat the cubs if they get a chance. But coyote daddies try to be nice and will even bring food to the babies if the mother should die.

"Elephant daddies just aren't home much," I said. "They stick around with their buddies. The fellows hang around together, and the ladies hang around together, but the daddies will come running if they are really needed."

*   *   *

Now that I was home, I was thoroughly enjoying my participation in Liz's language development. One day I was taking Elizabeth, then four, to the dentist. "We're going to see Dr. Jennings," I said.

"Why do you call him a doctor if he's a dentist?" she wanted to know.

"Because he studied a lot at college. He's a specialist, like a veterinarian."

"Oh," she said, proudly, "only special animals can go to him. Like me!"

Since animals quickly became our frame of reference, around the house I was frequently amazed at some of Liz's new concepts. From her I learned that "weasels" are little red spots that appear all over your face, and when that happens, you have to go to bed and call the doctor and you can't go to school.

"Why can't you go to school?" I asked. "Because weasels are catchy and you'd have a whole roomful of weasels," she exclaimed.

*   *   *

Eventually my father-in-law was enchanted with the idea of having his granddaughters, as well as his daughter, around.

"Is everything okay with you now?" he asked, as if it had been his idea to combine households and not mine. "I think I worked this out very well," he said smugly, "but I want you to be happy, son."

Meanwhile, we set up rules and regulations for our new order of our three-generation life together. Though the in-laws lived upstairs, Margaret and I would respect their privacy, and they would respect ours. We would phone to see if the other was in the mood for company. We would not just barge in; nor would they. Sunday dinner was the big deal, with everyone going upstairs to have Nanny Ida's superb spaghetti dishes.

Margy and I had our own sets of rules and regulations. She was to have some free days and a night out with her pals while I babysat. In fact, I was happy that she was enjoying a bit of life on her own, even though sometimes it seemed that I had to push her out the door. Eventually she was able to visit people and places, take a course, or see a movie with friends, relax and concentrate on the film, come back refreshed and guilt free.

As for me, I wrote out a credo in which I stated that a man, even though he is husband, father, and son-in-law, must also must be allowed "three hours a day in a locked room to think." Now I really understand cabin fever. All of us need a variety of outside activities. As a house person, I learned what it was like to crave privacy, and how important it was for both moms and dads to see new people on their own and to enjoy new situations.

The solution, as I see it, is for couples to write out their own credos, so that each can accept and know in advance what to expect of the other, easing tensions.

* * *

I knew that what I was doing was different. After all, I was making legal and sociological history. But I was unprepared for the tremendous amount of publicity I would receive. Reporters for all the major newspapers and wire services interviewed me to see what made me tick. Some came thinking it was just a stunt, but I hope most of them left convinced that it was no stunt and that I stand for paternity leave for *all* fathers and am ready to do whatever I can, testify before Congress, speak to women's groups, lobby state governments, whatever is necessary to bring it about.

What excited me even more than reporters probing my psyche and photographers snapping me bathing the baby or standing on my head with Liz, was the fact that serious students were writing papers, using me as an example of a unique father when addressing education and sociology conferences.

One such person, Barbara Gigante, began a paper entitled, "Father-Child: An Important Bond," with a quote from me: "It's vital that parents wake up to the reality that schools are not the primary instructional vehicles-parents are!"

A newspaper as far away as California carried a headline, Father Becomes Historic Paternity Leave Example. The article carefully explained that I had not sought paternity leave in order for my wife to go out and work. Quoting me, the story explained, "This was not done as a role reversal. It was done simply to enable me as a dad to participate fully in the development of my children."

The role of the father is often still misunderstood or fully appreciated in our society—even by me, but I'm working on it. At times, it does appear now that fathers are needed in certain situations more than previously thought.

For example, in Britain, a survey was made of 16,000 children to see whether the interest of the father had any measurable effect on the child's progress in school. One proof of a father's interest was his presence at parent-teacher meetings. It was found that children whose fathers accompanied their mothers to PTA meetings were on average seven months ahead in math and reading over those children whose fathers did not accompany the mothers to the meetings.

Then there was the study at Boston University's School of Education involving a hundred parents and their children. It was found by Audrey Stein, conductor of the study, that fathers are better at helping children who have language problems because they proved more versatile than mothers at adapting their own speech to the level of the particular child.

Only when my little girls, now eight and four, are grown up will we know how my experiment has turned out: when they can look back and evaluate it, and when educators and sociologists can evaluate them. But as far as I am concerned, if I can get one major thesis across to them, my four years' leave will not have been in vain.

What is my thesis?

I try to teach my kids that they are just a part of a big world that was here before they were born, and that will be here when they leave this world; that they are not alone, but are sharing the world with many living things, seen and unseen. They must do their best to enjoy life and to learn as much as possible about all the creatures of the world, not just themselves.

The reward is that from the animals they can learn new ways of doing things, some of which work for humans. They have already learned that knowledge is exciting and that learning new things makes life a game.

CHAPTER 3

The Orangutan Did It First

Any animal who happens to peek in the nursery window at a helpless newborn infant must have a good laugh. Compared with a human baby, a porcupine is practically an Einstein. It's born ready to fight. It can swat you with its tail or squirt you with needlepoint quills that will puncture your hide. A baby porcupine can not only stand up immediately, but can follow its mother. Not only that, it weans itself in one to two weeks and says good-bye to the old homestead, preferring to make its own way in the world.

A baby crocodile or alligator is pretty sharp, too. It can find its own food as soon as it's out of the egg. So can a fish. So can your average intelligent bug.

Let's see the progress of the human baby by comparison. Not till it's six to ten months old does a baby start to crawl. Walking usually doesn't take place until twelve to eighteen months.

On the other hand, think of how lucky you are compared with a parent mouse. The mouse is born blind. The mouse is born deaf. But the mouse and other mammalian animals can do something your human baby can't do—find their mothers' nipple. A human baby would starve at birth if its mother or some other kindhearted adult didn't guide it to a nipple.

How happy your average mother is when, after many months, her baby first puts its little arms around her neck and hangs on for a moment or two. But wait. Immediately after birth, a baby monkey, baboon, orangutan, chimpanzee, or gorilla can cling to its mother's neck or fur with strong hands and feet while mama swings from the trees. Human babies would be lost in a minute. Although Mother Nature, perhaps harking back to our monkey connection, still gives newborn babies a transitory strength to hold onto something. This ability is lost within hours and not regained for many months.

Little gorillas smile. Baby monkeys smile. Human babies smile. They're all special that way. And why do they do it? They get more attention that way. Baby smiles, everybody looks, beams, caters to baby, wanting to make it smile again.

Isn't a human baby showing intelligence even by sucking its mother's breast? Not really. The truth is that a baby will suck anything that touches its lips.

So will an orangutan.

Of all the creatures of the wild, the human baby resembles the great apes. The human baby resembles them even more than it resembles the baby monkey. There are studies in which lower baby primates have lived in human homes, worn diapers, played with toys, and drank from a baby bottle. The surprising thing is that the primate baby stays well ahead of the human baby for quite some time. Not until the primates and the human babies are between two and three years of age does the human baby start to pull ahead. Till then, the orangutan does it first, does it faster, does it better.

I hate to take you human parents down a peg, but do you realize that whatever your baby can do, some animal has you beat by a mile? Your baby could crawl at six months—four, five months early? Hurray! But did you know that a baby bison is born, gets up, and starts following its mother within a couple of hours?

Jenny, a young mother in the neighborhood, was bragging to Margy and me that her infant had actually reached for her breast with its hand and grasped her nipple at three months, less than half the time it took other babies to be able to use their hands in such a coordinated way.

"Isn't that amazing, she's almost as good as a koala bear," I said innocently. "But then, a koala bear has a special incentive to get to that nipple, climbing hand over hand as soon as it's born."

Little Liz, who is in love with the koala bear that appears in the TV commercial protesting that it hates the Australian Qantas Airlines, excitedly joined in to tell how clever the wee koala bear cub is, even though it is no bigger than a bumblebee at birth.

As soon as they are born, koala bears crawl up into their mama's pouch in search of food. It's a grim race for an important reason. There are not enough nipples in the mother's pouch to accommodate all the babies. So it is urgent that the little critters crawl like mad to get into the feedbag. The biggest and the strongest make it first and grab a treat for their own, swallowing it to make sure it is really theirs. The rest of the babies mill about and eventually fall to the ground and starve. Nature has made the decision. There's nothing the mother can do about it. The winners will hang on for two months. When they are ready in their development, they let go of the nipple and crawl out of the pouch to join their mama and take a look at the world.

What I'm saying is this—forget about setting world records. Don't pressure your baby. Let it develop at its own pace as other animals do. It will get around to the proper stage when its biological clock is good and ready. All you need to supply is love.

*   *   *

Can you and should you help a baby walk sooner? Marvin Gersh, a noted pediatrician in the 60's, refers to two groups of Hopi Indians, one of which carried their young on their backs, papoose style, until the age of one. The other followed the American system of letting the child crawl around. Both sets of children started walking at the same time despite the opposite methods used, about thirteen months.

It is love in the family environment that motivates a baby to want to crawl, to walk, and, eventually, to run to the loved ones. In an orphanage where the children could not get as much attention as they craved, the average baby did not crawl until it was twelve to fourteen or even fifteen months old. By the age of three, only fifteen percent could walk.

*   *   *

You say you're tired of how long it's taking to wean your baby? Tired because he wants your breast or a bottle months longer than your friend's baby of the same age? Well, relax, mums. Just be glad you're not a mother walrus. Its baby holds the record for the longest length of weaning time. The adolescent walrus isn't ready to quit feeding from its mother's breast for three years or so, until it's practically full-grown. The determining factor is teeth. A walrus can't stop nursing until its teeth get tough enough to crack the clams and mussels on which it will feed for the rest of its life.

In a way, the baby elephant deserves some sort of prize for suckling even longer, but the elephant does it as a treat. It is fully able to eat vegetation and survive on its own before it is a year old, but a baby elephant keeps suckling as long as it can get a little milk for dessert. Some baby elephants, like some human babies, won't try eating solid foods until their mamas nudge them into it.

*   *   *

It's really fascinating to compare the progress of human babies with the lesser animals. Let's take a look around. What could my babies, Elizabeth and Michelle, do at birth? Not much. They could move their heads slightly and move their eyes from side to side.

I was surprised to find out that human babies react to the color red, and follow it with their eyes. On the other hand, most everybody knows that bulls do not see the red of the cape that the bullfighter waves at them. They are angered not by the color, but by the taunting gesture made with the cape. Human babies are among the few mammals of the world to see color. All the primates see color too, the monkeys and the apes and all their cousins. Dogs, of course, don't see color. They're not primates. When you get to fish and insects and birds, you again get creatures that are blessed with color-sensing ability. In fact, there is a particular fish who inspects her babies very closely at birth and memorizes them by the exact position and color of their spots. Thereafter, she knows her own young.

And speaking of recognizing their young, I have concluded that taking babies from mothers immediately after birth in hospitals is bad. There is evidence that babies, too, recognize something of their mother when they are born. Dr. Lee Salk, for one, was convinced that they know their own mother's heartbeat. Doctors are finding that newborns are happier when the sound of their mother's heartbeat or the smell of their mother remains constantly around them. In experiments, it was found that a recording of a mother's heartbeat caused newborn babies in the maternity ward to cry less.

After little Michelle was born, Elizabeth, who was three years and ten months old, wanted to know why the doctor holds a baby upside down at birth. I found out then that not only Liz, but also all her friends, thought a baby could not start to breathe unless it was held upside down and spanked. I corrected their misconception, explaining that a human baby is held upside down mainly to let any mucous in the mouth run out.

"So why do they spank the baby?" asked Sammy, one of the little wise guys of the neighborhood. "It hasn't done anything yet."

"Ha Ha," I laughed weakly. "To help it start breathing. It probably would anyway, but they do it to help. Does that answer your question, Sammy?" I could see he was working up to another try. "Do the other animals spank their babies to make them breathe?" he asked, giggling at his six-year-old cleverness.

"Well, you almost got me again," I said, "but the whales give their babies what you might call a little spank. They have to bounce them up from the ocean into the air to help them start breathing."

Then I held the whole neighborhood of little ones spellbound as I told them a really startling thing. "Would you believe," I began, "that the mother rat has to teach her baby rats to go to the bathroom? The mother tickles their tummies with her tongue when she is washing them after they are born, and that gets them started. After that they can go all by themselves."

They all looked at me in disbelief and awe. But it was Sammy again who rose to the occasion. "It's a good thing nobody tried to tickle my tummy," he said, sounding mighty disgusted. "I'd have fixed 'em."

"What would you have done?" I asked, curiously. "I'd have smashed 'em." He made a big fist and swatted the air.

"Then you must have been a baby baboon or maybe a monkey," I told him, to the merriment of my little troop. "Because human babies can't use their hands or feet for months. It took three months for baby Liz over here to discover she had hands and feet, and it took her another month to discover there were two hands."

"How did I found out?" Liz wanted to know. "You found out because you clapped them," I said. "That's how you found out. You clapped them, and one hand held onto the other. You were really surprised."

It was the end of the lecture. I had lost my audience, who were now playing follow-the-leader around the house.

*   *   *

Let's return a moment to a subject I was speaking about before, the visual abilities of a newborn baby. At birth, an infant can see objects, though not in detail. Scientific experiments using rear-view screens show that the infant fears large objects and is terrified of things that seem to be moving toward it rapidly.

At three months, or four, the baby recognizes various objects and surely knows that Mama is not Aunt Marie.

At birth, an orangutan already knows that Aunt Marie is not Mama.

I'm not trying to put down parents who have great pride in their children's achievements so much as I am trying to make them aware of, and have greater respect for, our various talented animal relatives. Well, maybe I am putting down humans a little, but I figure they can take it.

You think your kid can run pretty fast, and you hope he grows up and joins the elite list of runners who will take part in a marathon. Well, he may crack the human record, but I doubt that he'll ever outrace the cheetah, the fastest land animal in the world. A cheetah can run seventy miles per hour, and at top speed, only one foot is on the ground at any time. She's cracked the one-minute mile!

But the cheetah is still not the fastest living creature, only the fastest land animal. The record on air flight goes to the duck hawk, which has been clocked at 180 miles per hour.

Cheetahs, eat your hearts out!

*   *   *

You think you have given birth to a big baby? You have been writing on those birth announcements that your little precious has made family history by weighing in at 10½ pounds? Well, you don't know what big is. If a blue whale could write a birth announcement, it would say that Junior has arrived and is just an average baby— seven tons.

*   *   *

People like to mention two things when telling why the human child is superior to the animal—toilet training and the fact that human children take care of their parents in their old age.

Well, I know a lot of children who did not grow up and take care of their parents. We'll get to the animal's side of that in a minute. But first, let's look at toilet training.

Most animals are very careful not to dirty their own nests. Even birds train their young to place their feces on the rim of the nest as soon as they are old enough to comprehend it. The parent birds then pick up any deposits and fly them to a place away from the nest, dropping them to the ground.

Margy was very proud when she had Michelle trained to use her potty exclusively in a little over two years. "It isn't all that great," I said, "when you consider that it took Michelle twenty four months to do what a bird does in less than a week!"

"Is that so?" asked Margy.

"Sure is," I said. "Most birds are no more than five days old when their mothers have them trained to put their droppings on a precise spot on the rim of the nest. She's very fussy about this. If they forget and put their deposit in the middle of the nest, she gives their little rear ends a sharp pinch to remind them. It doesn't take too many reminders."

Bees, too, keep the hives clean and sweet and throw the feces out of the nest. Honeybees back out of the hive and let their feces, consisting of uric acid crystals, fall over the side. All the world at that moment is their outhouse. They don't need a mama bird to do it for them. They do it themselves.

Margy and I were amused. We had not pushed Michelle in her toilet training. There is nothing wrong at all with waiting until a child is two years old or more before toilet training begins. If the child is angry or upset by it, as Michelle would be now and then, stop pushing and wait awhile longer. Mother Nature has programmed into each child a personal biorhythm that will take over, and give the child the strength and desire to control his or her urinary and excretory functions.

When we were training baby Michelle at somewhere around two, we made a game of it and had what we called "Michelle's corner" where we placed her potty. Michelle got to sit in her corner several times a day, and we made a big fuss about it if something appeared in the pot. Eventually, Michelle got the idea and was very proud to run to her corner any time she got the urge, all on her own. When she came to get us, Margy and I would say, "Oh, we're going to Michelle's corner. Let's see what is in Michelle's corner."

One day Michelle called us as usual, and when we got to Michelle's corner there was a little pile right on the rug. Margy and I looked at each other and couldn't help but burst out laughing, "I had taken the potty away to sterilize it," said Margy. We were so busy talking about Michelle's corner we forgot to mention the corner was important because the potty sat there.

*   *   *

Now that other point—the care and feeding of one's parents after they are senior citizens.

It's very rare that animals take care of their elders, but this is the case with termites. Whatever else you may say about the dreaded creatures that can destroy your home, your nerves, and your bank account, they are good to their mothers! When termites are first born, their mothers regurgitate the food that the babies need. Eventually, it's the other way around. Young termites eat wood, transforming it into predigested food, and regurgitate some to feed their parents.

And it isn't just bugs who show so much consideration. The wild dog also throws up partially digested food to feed the old folks, if they are too slow to run with the pack. The old folks, standing in front of the den to receive this bounty, are most grateful. They put their front paws forward and bow their heads low in a twisted position saying, "Please" and "Thank you," as they no doubt have taught their youngsters to do against the day they're old too.

CHAPTER 4

Feeding Time at Our Zoo

Even the animals would not be so cruel as the parents and pediatricians of the 40's. When a kitten meows, whether it is a house cat or Bengal tiger, the mother cat pays attention, sniffs out the trouble with its nose, and makes little purring "now, now" noises to reassure it.

The reason everybody turned to Dr. Benjamin Spock in the 50's and 60's was that he had the courage to define abusing your child. Let him set his own timetable. Eventually Spock had a reputation for excessive permissiveness, but it only seemed excessive compared to the rigidity that had gone before.

My theory? I think children are as varied as the animals of the wild and must be treated in an individual way, with only one constant—love in large quantity.

* * *

When should your child eat? When he or she is hungry. Some children are like birds who must eat in small quantities all the time. As long as the food is healthy and not too fattening—fruit, raw carrots, meats, and cereals, what's the difference? The child can still join the family at the dinner table and have another nibble and conversation.

Like the mole, which lines its tunnel with worms for its future feedings, Michelle requires something to eat every few hours.

I know one woman who is sure her child is going to starve because he does not eat a big breakfast, or lunch, and only seems interested in food at dinner. I assured her that the lion in the wild manages to stay king of the jungle, even though he doesn't have breakfast either and only gulps down a hearty meal every other day or so.

At our house, when there is company, we all sit up straight and eat politely. But when it's just our private zoo, we play a game of guess who I am. Who I am is a different animal every time, and anything goes short of throwing food on the floor or over one's shoulder, as the elephant does.

It is hilarious to watch the little ones' contortions to demonstrate a particular animal eating. Yet, if I should say, "Simon says, 'Human!' Company coming!" Liz will suddenly snap to and hold her fork as delicately as Jacqueline Kennedy Onassis.

How do the animals eat? Lizards use their long tongue. Try watching a kid do that without breaking up. No hands, just a long tongue. Anteaters use their long noses. So do the elephants, and Elizabeth uses a long arm to imitate the pick-up abilities of its long, mobile trunk. A giraffe spreads its legs and stretches its long neck down to pick vegetation from a low spot. A giraffe baby is the most completely developed mammal at birth, a complete miniature, with horns, tail, and tassel, ready to stretch its long neck, too.

Snakes swallow food whole and sometimes pick on something too big to handle. Liz can act this out to perfection, wriggling and squirming with that eloquent arm as the snake holding a chicken leg who swallowed the whole chicken. "No," she says, "I swallowed a whole deer, and the antlers are killing me. Ugh."

"Well, what kind of snake are you?" I ask, testing her.

"I'm a python," she roars, proud to know which snake could swallow such a big dinner. She learned this fact from a wondrous picture book of true things about the world and its slightly weird inhabitants, *Strange As It Seems* by John Hix.

The next day, it is Michelle who is baffling us all by daintily wrapping a piece of bread in her napkin and then putting it between her shoes and rubbing it between her feet.

"This is the most mystifying performance I have ever seen," I tell her, "and I will give a silver dollar to anyone who can guess what animal Michelle is and what she's doing."

Even Mother Margy, who is pretty good at reading Michelle's mind, is stumped. Finally, we get it out of her. She's a horseshoe crab and she's chewing her food with her legs, the only creature on this green earth to do such a wacky thing. Not bad for a four-year-old.

Michelle's specialty, however, is imitating the little nibblers of the animal kingdom. She will perch herself on her chair on her knees, with her two little hands tight against her body and in front of her, showing how raccoons wash their food.

Not only have the children learned how the animals eat, but they have learned what they eat and what is good and nutritious about that food and diet. Believe me, a child will be much more interested in learning which vitamins an elephant is getting in its grass than what humans get from the salad at the dinner table.

The children have learned from the animals that it is certainly not good to overeat. One overweight dog in the neighborhood hates to run and play and wheezes like an old man. What is even worse, the kids learned from the newspapers (we always read news of animals aloud) that two of the three offspring of a lesser panda died of overeating because their mother had died and had not been around to supervise their feedings.

The girls know that some juvenile animals are smart and develop good judgment about how much to eat while others don't know when to quit. So far they are impressed enough to be careful of their own intake. I am very pleased that they don't take a second piece of candy or cake, even if their little friends do.

Their reward is praise from us. We tell them that we noticed their restraint and we tell them how nice and trim they look. We do not give food as rewards, we give books, coins, toys, and praise.

Elizabeth is a meat eater like a lion or tiger, but Michelle is almost a vegetarian, wolfing down salad like an antelope eats hay and grass.

Michelle hardly touches meat. We don't worry about it. All the nutriments in meat can also be found in vegetables, eggs, and cheese. Hundreds of thousands of children are born in vegetarian families and grow up to be just as healthy as meat eaters.

It is amazing to see how large and healthy the strict vegetarians of the animal kingdom can become. The gorilla, who is the largest of the great apes, subsists on all the green leaves and stalks he can strip from the trees and bushes. The elephant is the largest of the land animals and prefers straw and grass, thank you. Even Seattle Slew, that great champion of racing horses, made racing history on a diet of oats and hay. What I am trying to say is that, if they were animals, Elizabeth would probably be a tiger or lion and Michelle might be the racehorse.

If birds don't get the right food, their feathers do not grow strong during the period of deprivation and can be brittle and break. A baby's bones can also become defective from lack of calcium and various vitamins.

Animals sense what they need. Certain plants seem to have medicinal values. Even meat-eating animals, like the cat family, seek out certain plants when they don't feel well. Liz says, "That shows mother earth is their doctor."

We have decided to follow the ways of the wild and not force our own little animals to eat foods that are distasteful. Nor is it terribly important to always have a greatly varied diet. Many animals eat only a few select foods. Like the four-footed animals, little human animals feel instinctively a hunger for foods they need.

Sometimes, one or the other is hungry for fish, and I think it must be a need for iron expressing itself. At another time, one is hungry for citrus fruits; this could signal need for more vitamin C.

In the animal kingdom, it's the offspring who is delighted to get food. In our human kingdom, the parent is the one who is most delighted when the child eats. Many parents act as if their children are on the verge of starvation and stuffing them with foods for which they have an aversion. For some reason, the carrot is the villain to most children. Yet that is the food that many mothers insist that their children eat with great regularity.

* * *

Animals don't beg their offspring to eat beyond their capacity. Only the birds try to stuff their young ones with food and they have a special reason—a bird must eat its weight in bugs or seeds every day. That takes a lot of fetching and hauling on the part of the weary parents.

There is also a sinister aspect to that touching picture of papa and mama bird returning over and over to stuff those bugs and worms into the little birds' open mouths. The little birds better keep those mouths open if they want to stay alive. If the mother bird returns with a worm and the baby bird keeps its mouth closed to show it's had enough, the parent may push the little one right out of the nest to its destruction because it assumes the little one is sick. This is a nasty way to treat a child, but not having medicine, the mama bird is protecting the rest of her brood from contamination.

*   *   *

Paternity leave meant not only that I was home, but that I was underfoot. At first I tried to be the leader, the boss. All I wanted was to be everything to both daughters, to my wife, and to the neighborhood. I was all over the place. Margy did not want a job outside the home. "All I want is to raise my kids the Italian way," she said. "I'm just an Italian mother."

"Fine," I said. "Just do what you like and forget I'm around, unless you need me. I'm here to help."

"Okay," she said, "make a cup of pasta for Elizabeth."

I measured a cup of pasta and put it on to cook. Only after it had boiled out on the stove did I think to read the directions and find out that to make a cup of something refers to the size of the finished product.

I'll never forget the first time I tried to put a spoon in Michelle's mouth. Michelle was not opening her mouth for me. Even when I told her four-monthold eminence that it was "dee-lish-eeous, yummy, yummy."

As I put the spoon to her mouth, she turned her head.

After Elizabeth had watched my performance for a while in amused tolerance, she said, "Oh, Daddy, you can't do it that way. You have to use the flying spoon."

She took the spoon and waved it all around, chattering away and telling how the flying spoon was coming to Michelle. Michelle opened wide. We were in business.

Spock says forget flying spoons. Gersch too says forget flying spoons. But I say a little dining drama never hurt anyone. I see nothing wrong with little games, as long as the parent does not plead with a child to eat. Animals, too, play little games with their infants, sometimes pretending to leave them alone. The little cub then gets on with it and appreciates the food that much more.

Actually, the problem of how to feed the baby arrives even before the baby does. It's the one question women ask the pediatrician, the other women in the waiting room and their own friends. In fact, it is the question the expectant mother asks everyone. Should mothers breastfeed their babies? As long as the baby gets plenty of cuddling, it shouldn't matter how it gets its food supply. But nothing compares to breastmilk. Artists have made idealized versions of breast feeding. Husbands like to see it. It's beautiful. Even the pets in the house enjoy being part of this circle of love.

*   *   *

How do animals treat the dinner hour if they are mammals? Not too tenderly. Some animals make the baby run after it to catch hold of a teat when it is hungry, especially if the baby has been around a while and the mother is getting a little bored with being pestered for food. Human solicitude is touching.

What about eating schedules, feeding schedules? Unfortunately, I was born at the time when it was believed that babies should be made to conform to a timetable-food every four hours and not a minute earlier, no matter how the baby cried. Children were not to be picked up if they cried. It would spoil the baby, and besides, crying strengthened the lungs. Was it any wonder that I and so many children cried themselves into colic?

Thank goodness child experts have now relented, but even if they hadn't, I would believe that the only timetable is love. No child of ours cries in a crib without being picked up or soothed and talked to or all three. For some reason, hardened adults have an idea that a helpless child is crying simply just to get attention. It doesn't take a great brain to figure out that, if a child is crying in his or her crib, one of four things is wrong: the baby is hungry, in pain or wet, lonely, or, yes, even afraid.

Just relax and let nature take its course. You don't have to defend your baby's eating habits to anyone. This isn't an eating contest for babies. Your normal baby knows what it wants and when it wants it, and it is not shy about letting you know.

* * *

At the dinner table, our family can be downright boisterous, imitating animals and their feeding habits. The girls have a set of rules on how to eat when they visit friends or their grandparents. The rules they have memorized are:

1. Sit up straight and hold your neck up tall like a giraffe.
2. Pass things nicely and don't throw them like a monkey.
3. Chew with your mouth closed and don't make noises like an otter.
4. Remember to use your fork and don't go feeding your face like a raccoon.
5. Use your napkin to wipe your mouth and don't lick your paws or wash your face like a cat.

At our own dinner table, we all wait till the last one is finished so that nobody has to feel pushed to eat fast. We tried it the other way, with Elizabeth being permitted to leave the table and run to play with her friends, but Michelle would not eat any more, wanting to follow her, or would become all tensed up. It was much friendlier and relaxing for everyone to sit around talking while the slowest finished.

* * *

The children are always fascinated to know what food the various animals eat, for example: which eat meat, grasses, mice or worms, and which sometimes steal their dinner from others. They even knew that a congressman, Andrew Jacobs, Jr., had a Great Dane named C-5, who he taught to be a vegetarian.

While visiting the Staten Island Zoo one day, Elizabeth had a talk with the zookeeper about what animals should and should not eat. He said that it was shameful that animals were eating leather gloves and cigars and candy and shoelaces because people were throwing these things to them.

He said that the kindest thing Elizabeth and her friends could do was to follow the policy of not feeding a zoo animal at all, even if the animal seemed to be begging, and the children wanted to share their bag of goodies with them.

"What does the monkey eat?" asked Elizabeth.

She learned that the zoo mixes a special formula of vegetables, greens, and vitamins added to a commercial monkey chow mix, that anyone could buy for their own pets.

"What does the lion eat?" she next wanted to know.

The average lion, she learned, eats a giant portion of meat, about thirty-five pounds a meal.

"Why can't I help feed the animals?" asked little Liz. "I used to help feed my little sister when she was a little baby. I used the flying spoon."

I was afraid that we had overstayed our welcome, but the zookeeper laughed and told Liz what had happened at the big zoo in Washington, D.C., when the zoo tried to bring about public participation. The animal keepers passed out chunks of fish to the people watching the seals, and told them they could throw it to the cavorting seals.

The fish was wrapped in a paper towel, which people were told to remove before throwing the fish to the seals. But no matter how often the zoo people reminded the public, they continued to throw the fish, paper towel and all. The worst part of this was the seals were eating and enjoying it.

"Why didn't they give the people the fish without the paper towel?" Elizabeth asked with perfect logic.

"Because people don't like to touch fish, I'm afraid," said the zookeeper sadly, "so they just had to give up public participation."

Liz was all excited again. She had just remembered another question she wanted to ask: "What does the blue whale eat?" Since she knows the blue whale is the largest of them all, and a mammal like herself, she found this of great interest.

"It eats krill," he said. "That's a little fellow that looks a lot like shrimp. So you can imagine how many the whale has to eat at every mouthful. He is like a bulldozer shoveling them in."

*   *   *

The most delightfully creatures that we like to watch while they eat are the otters, and the children have spent many happy hours eating a meal otter fashion. Sea otters, made of sturdier stuff than we, cavort in the icy Aleutians. In Staten Island, New York, our mimicking can only be done in the summer in the backyard in a pool.

Fortunately, we have a not so fancy one, but a huge plastic pool with a platform around it and stairs for climbing up. Such as it is, it suits our little otters fine. The way you eat like an otter is that you lie on your back in the water-rubber rafts or inner tubes are permitted and you use your chest as a table.

Naturally, when you are an otter, you eat fish or seafood. King crab is quite acceptable. If you could find a sea urchin, that would be the supreme treat, and, if you could afford it, abalone would also be very nice. It is said by fishermen that otters eat abalone each day, which makes for a very expensive diet and puts otters them a little out of reach in our household. At any rate, most fish taste best when fried and then stuffed into one's mouth, otter fashion, with both hands.

But the best part of being an otter is all the noise you can make. The children saw a Cousteau documentary showing how noisily the otter ate its dinner while rocking along on its back on the waves; the girls were absolutely delighted to follow suit. Smack, smack, crunch, crunch. Oh, how noisily the otter and his loyal fans, Liz and Michelle, tackled their food while in the pool.

The otter, you may be sure, has become Mother Margy's least favorite animal for setting an example for her children. She would rather see the little girls imitate the neat and silent eaters of the animal kingdom, like the busy bee who dips so neatly into the saucer of a flower, never wasting a drop of nectar.

Michelle wanted to be a bird and fly in the sky all by herself until she found out from Elizabeth that birds actually eat worms. She would have to eat worms! And bugs!

"I can't be a bird," she said, almost in tears. But when I checked into the matter, taking the girls with me to the local library, we discovered that some birds like Michelle were also repelled by the worms and only ate seeds.

Goldfinches, we found out, crack dandelion seeds and think they are dandy. But what impressed the girls most was that a bird, the hawk finch, has such a strong beak it can crack cherry pits and eat the seeds inside.

Appealing to her four-year-old sense of fairness, since birds eat so many bugs, Michelle viewed it as some kind of poetic justice that one bug is actually able to eat a bird—the giant bird-eating spider of South America. It jumps on birds that are feeding on the ground.

* * *

Strangely enough, the girls are most interested not in the dainty eaters of the animal kingdom, but in the roughest and toughest. They want to know, for example, how the snake can kill and eat something. I explained that some snakes catch and choke the wind out of their catch by wrapping themselves around the prey, squeezing it so it can't breathe. Other snakes inject venom into the creatures they catch to stun or kill them. But in either case, the snakes just swallow the animals whole.

"Doesn't the bad snake get poisoned too?" asked Liz.

"No," I replied, "evidently it is immune to its own poison just as we humans are immune to some of the germs within our own body."

Though a snake can swallow large chunks of food whole, the girls have been cautioned never to imitate this phase of a snake's eating habit, because of the danger of choking. Still, Liz managed to convey an image of a snake eating when she slithered up to a jelly bean lying on a napkin on the floor and wiggled as she picked it up with her lips, wiggling some more to show that the jelly bean was sliding all the way through her body.

It's fantastic that all creatures of the world do not compete for the same food, and that what one likes, another may detest. Liz cannot believe that one animal, the aardvark, from the Pink Panther show, lives on ants and thinks they are the greatest delicacy in the world. Neither can she believe that termites can digest wood thinking it has an excellent flavor. She feels sorry that the cow who gives all that nice milk is happy to settle for a diet of nothing more than "plain dumb grass," and will even eat it when it's all dry and hard in a form known as hay.

But she really shook her head in disbelief when she learned from her hero, Jacques Cousteau, that a toothless sort of animal, the manatee, can live for years on nothing but water hyacinths that lie on the surface of the swampy waters of Florida. "It's silly," she said. "Nobody goes around eating flowers."

"Well, then, you're even," I said. "The manatee hasn't heard of your crazy diet either."

"How do you know?" she asked.

"Because he told me so, you silly."

*   *   *

CHAPTER 5

Don't Monkey Around with a Kangaroo

In our time, protection of the young and of the old is very important. Naturally, we are teaching our girls everything they should know about protecting themselves as they go about living in a big city. It takes the concern away from the lessons that must be learned, to talk about and imitate how the animals defend themselves and their young.

The kangaroo rates high at our house, especially the female kangaroo. She's the original bionic woman. She can jump more than thirty feet in one graceful leap. She can jump to the roof of a one-story house, or skip the roof and land on the branch above it.

The kangaroo is a sweet gentle creature who eats plants and minds her own business. But, should anyone get too familiar with her babies, called joeys, she sits back on her haunches with all the dignity her seven-foot height can give her and swats the intruder mighty blow with a forepaw which Muhammad Ali would envy. In fact, she's been known to disembowel a foe with one karate chop.

If that isn't enough, she can be equally convincing with her tail, but normally uses it to sit on, or to give balance as she comes bounding out of a fifty-foot tree.

It's amazing that this Amazon who weighs as much as 200 pounds gives birth to babies that are no bigger than an inch, and are completely helpless. But even mama kangaroo, strong as she is, doesn't trust herself completely to protect her babies, especially if she knows that a pack of wild dogs is closing in for an attack. She hides her babies under some leaves before she goes into battle or attempts to outrace the pack. Then when all is calm, she returns to find her young.

This demonstrates to my kids that even though mommy and daddy are big and strong, sometimes bad people work together to harm children or take their possessions, and so we must take precautions to protect them, locking doors of the house and car and such.

Taking a tip from the kangaroo, when my little ones are old enough, I will send them to class to learn karate, jujitsu, or, any sport that make one quick on one's feet and able to duck from danger.

* * *

Speech undoubtedly started as a warning of danger.

I've read that Einstein didn't talk until he was between three and four. He just hadn't found any use for words until then. Some animals communicate to let each other know of a threat from the outer world—a low growl, bared teeth, or even a raised tail. We have had a lot of fun around the house trying to talk like the animals, and, sometimes, sure enough, it turned away the anger. Once when Liz was angry, I told her to tell me about it in snake language. She hissed so effectively that she forgot what she was angry about.

The direction of the wag of a dog's tail speaks with great eloquence. Up and down means, "I'm guilty, I'm guilty, don't punish me." Side to side means, "Isn't this wonderful, I'm so happy."

Beavers slap the water with their tails to warn of danger. That's heavy talking. Even heavier are those creatures who speak with what's under their tails. The skunk, for example, throws a powerful jet of vile-smelling liquid. But skunks are not the only ones; they've just developed the worst reputation.

There's a caterpillar that's safe from all enemies because as soon as an enemy approaches, the caterpillar's scent gland releases a foul-smelling substance that helps the enemy decide that it's suddenly not hungry. From a safe distance, the enemy notices that the swallowtail caterpillar is staring with a vengeful eye, making and the enemy move further away. But it's all a sham. The eyes are not real, but simply nature's markings providing a further defense against the dreaded birds. Nature is certainly wonderful in its infinite variety of protections for the weak.

You might think the zebra is unlucky in having such vibrant black and white stripes, but in its native habitat among tall grasses, the markings blend right in with the light and shadow under the trees. It is said that a person can be very close to a herd of zebra and not even notice them.

* * *

Would you believe that among the most vicious fighters for a lady's hand is the creature who has such a great reputation for gentleness, the bunny rabbit. When the fight ends with one rabbit limping away, there is blood and gore everywhere. It is more than likely that both of them have ears that have been ripped open.

You would think that the lady in question would want nothing to do with either of these tattered and wretched creatures, but such is certainly not the case. She seems quite happy to prove the human adage, "To the victor belong the spoils."

The vicuna male doesn't even have to fight to convince his herd that he's bigger and better than everyone. Showing real intelligence, he knows that if he stands on a rock he looks more imposing than anyone else, so that is just what he does. It is seldom that one of the bachelors in the territory dare challenge him. He's king of the castle.

As for protecting that castle, he's got teeth and a good kick. He will run bravely between the enemy and his wives and kids, and he will sound a vocal alarm to get the help of the other males. But he's not a mean creature, and he's not looking for trouble. Trouble has to look for him.

That's the way it is with the elephant, too. Female elephants hardly ever have a fight. They usually stick together as a group and are very peaceful. But when two females happen to take a dislike to each other and cannot get along, watch out. They have been known to bite off the other's tail.

If two male elephants happen to come to blows, it is a much more serious matter, and the ground shakes. It is a fight to the finish. They will lock trunks and try to get the other impaled on their long tusks which can kill as nicely as a rapier.

If they should fail in the tug of war, they lunge at each other, and one sometimes succeeds in ripping open the whole side of the other, disemboweling him and leaving him dying.

And what was it all about? Jealousy over a female. If it were a real battle against outside enemies, the females would be the major warriors, charging and trampling the enemy.

*   *   *

We have done a lot of studying at our house to find out what various animals do to escape an enemy. I remember one day when Liz didn't want to go outside and walk down the sidewalk to her girlfriend's house because, as she put it, "There's a bad boy out there."

Together we checked the animal books and our memories of past explorations into animal life to see how all the animals handle fear. The octopus spits dye and darts away through the haze. Does— does Liz want to do that? No.

The kangaroo would go out there and punch the boy with fists and a mean tail. Does Liz want to do that? No.

The snail and the turtle stay put and hide in their shells until they feel safe again. But that means waiting. Elizabeth does not want to wait. She wants to go to the corner now. She has a great idea. Some fish change colors; she could put on her Halloween costume so the boy won't recognize her as she runs past.

No, she decides, that's too hard, and she's not that afraid of him. "I'm just going to be a dog," she says, "I think maybe a French poodle, and walk by, very friendly, and smile at him. But I won't stick out my tongue. I'm only half dog."

So little Liz solved her problem. But she also knows that she need not be ashamed to run away from a dangerous situation. Even the largest animals don't always stay and fight; they sometimes run for their lives. Sometimes they simply leave because they'd rather not fight that day.

Humans are certainly not the only creatures who rise loyally to the defense of their weaker members. In fact, humans could take lessons in courage from many creatures, some of them lowly. Consider the little termites. When they see the enemy approaching, their soldiers quickly surround the defenseless young members of the colony to give them time to escape, even though many of the soldiers are gobbled up as a result. They refuse to save themselves first.

Man has been copying nature for many years in learning the art of self-defense. By studying the animals, Liz and Michelle are starting to get an inkling of what war is all about. Already they know that if people copied the right kind of animals, animals like the manatee that are gentle and loving and do not know anything about fighting, there would be no wars.

But they know that the world is not ready to follow the manatee yet, and so they must be wise in the ways of the real world. We have sat around seeing if we could figure out all the reasons that any creatures in the wild fight and we've come up with quite a list:

> To get a mate that another animal also wants
> To protect itself
> To protect its children
> Because it's hungry and it wants to kill for food

The animals are great teachers of every kind of defense. Animals kick, claw, bite, scratch, gouge, stomp, and run and hide. The versatility with which animals find ways to protect themselves is amazing, and so are the weapons they find. A skunk's spray can blind a man temporarily. But deep down a skunk is really a nice little animal unless feeling cornered. Then it bends its head forward, lifts its backside, points with its rear end, and shoots two streams of yellow liquid from its anal glands. What comes out is a liquid with odor is so horrible that strong men clutch their noses and choke and bury their clothes to get rid of the stench, if even a drop has gotten on them.

Sickening as the skunk musk is, another animal has a still more obnoxious defense. Strangely enough, that animal is the elegant mink, famous for its beautiful coats. People might change their feelings about this creature if they could see the mink as it rises to its own defense, dropping an aerosol bomb that makes the skunk's musk seem like sweet perfume. The only redeeming grace about the mink is that at least it cannot spray its asphyxiating musk as far as a skunk can. It must settle for dropping its "little gift" right where it stands.

I have explained to Elizabeth that children who will not take a bath for long periods of time and smell very bad are like the little mink and the skunk who use their odor as a defense against people.

Poison is another clever way Mother Nature arms certain little creatures of the world to defend themselves. Some snakes use poison. The poison of a black widow spider can kill. The poison of a bee can also kill some people who are allergic to it, or even a perfectly normal person if there are enough bee stings.

The sad thing is that, even if it is only defending itself, the bee that stings loses its life in the process.

What is less known is that even friendly-looking little mammals can kill with poison. The poison of the tiny short-tailed shrew has been compared to that of the cobra. The shrew uses its poison sometimes to defend itself and sometimes to kill a larger creature, such as a mouse, for food.

What happens is that the poison slows the mouse's heart causing it to faint. It never recovers consciousness and soon becomes the shrew's dinner.

Many animals, primates and the cat family, use a display of ferocious teeth to help frighten away enemies.

Many four-footed animals rely on their legs for both running and kicking. A horse's hoof can kill a man, and so can the kick of a deer.

Many animals display their protective devices at the other end of their bodies—their heads. Musk oxen, faced with danger, lower their heads and rely on their fierce horns to stem the attack.

Many animals run or hide as their protection, and I have told my little girls, as well as little boys of the neighborhood, that there is no shame in running and hiding until danger has passed. They are only doing what a squirrel or fox or any other of dozens of animals would do.

When one little boy said shamefacedly, "I don't want to be chicken," I told him that there is no shame in being called "chicken" because among the fiercest creatures of the world are the fighting game cocks. I told him that these little male chickens are so fierce that sometimes they will stay and fight until one or the other is dead.

Liz was interested in a moth that stands upside down and "makes like a leaf" to fool the enemy.

Actually, there is many an animal through evolution which has developed protection with camouflage coloring. Many fish look like the bottom of the ocean, or like stones, or like weeds. Many insects look like bark of a tree, or like flowers. But the most famous of the camouflage creatures is the chameleon, a lizard who actually has the power to change its own color to blend in with whatever is around it.

I have compared children who are excessively shy with the creatures who camouflage themselves. "They don't like bright colors or anything that looks different or distinctive, and they try to blend into the environment."

"Am I like that?" asked Lizzy.

I had to laugh. "I'll let you answer that question yourself. Do you remember when you wanted me to paint your face like a clown so that you could dress up in a funny costume and jump out at people when it wasn't even Halloween?"

"Yes, it was my birthday. I had a lot of fun."

"I rest my case."

Elizabeth had a question, "How does a bat protect itself?"

"Mostly by broken field flying," I said, "and staying away from a predatory bird that is out to get it." I explained that the bat can track any dangerous creature around it by sending out radar signals at the rate of 90,000 vibrations per second.

"But I mean what does a bat do to protect itself if you catch it?" pursued Liz.

"Scratches like hell," I said.

"Oh, oh, you said a four-letter word. That's a no, no," scolded Liz. "You have to put two cents in the kitty."

"This course in self-defense is costing me money," I said, digging out the pennies for Liz to drop in the "Cussing Box."

Liz's friend, Margo, had joined us, and Liz was recounting the many ways an animal can protect itself, ending up with the amazing speed of the cheetah, that seventy-mile-per-hour "bionic" creature.

"But you didn't say the deer," said Margo. "The deer is fast, too, and that's how it protects itself as it runs away. One even jumped over our Mustang. Daddy says the deer is the fastest animal in the world."

Liz was rising to my defense, "No it isn't. My daddy knows everything."

"Yes, it is. Yes, it is. Yes, it is."

Was this shaping into a real fight? "Girls," I said, "I'm glad you care enough about the truth to get excited. You see, I didn't make it up. You consult books, you consult experts. Brains are our defense. Use them!" I grabbed both little ones and playfully tapped their heads together as they giggled, and all made up.

"I know one other way that an animal protects itself and I'll bet nobody can guess," teased Liz.

She was right, we couldn't think of another way, and I thought she was up to her old tricks with her riddles. But I was mistaken. "You forgot the owl," she screamed.

"What does the owl do that's different," I asked. Liz answered, "it sleeps all day so nobody can find it, and that's its protection."

"And you're just lucky that somebody loves you," I shot back, "and that's your protection."

CHAPTER 6

Thankfully I'm Not a Sea Horse

I agree with the authorities who say it is bad to counter the question, "How was I born?" with all kinds of stories of birds and bees and alligators and little fish. The child isn't asking about little fish; he's asking about little humans.

If you are perfectly frank in answering questions as they are asked about human babies, you run the risk that some children will go so far as to ask the parents to "show me how you make a baby."

"What do you mean?" I said, stalling for time when it happened to me.

"How do you put the seed in Mommy?" fouryear-old Elizabeth asked matter-of-factly. "So the baby can come out of her pagina."

"Well, I'd be happy to," I said, "Just get me a piece of paper and Mommy and I will draw a picture for you."

When a child finally gets around to asking about the exact mechanics of intercourse, draw a medical-type picture of a vagina and a penis in position, and explain that the seed passes from the male to the female into the uterus where it is protected and will develop into a beautiful baby.

My artwork was so dull that Elizabeth soon had switched to eggs and was drawing Easter eggs and ostrich eggs. In fact, she hauled out her little picture book which shows how a chicken embryo develops and hatches and soon was telling me the story of how life comes about. "You see, Daddy, here is the picture after four days, and there is the heart and it is starting to beat and in two weeks it hatches."

"Well, that's the story for the chicken and her egg, but about this ostrich egg you made here that covers the whole page, did you know that is the biggest egg in the whole world and it takes three times longer to hatch?"

Now she was giggling. "I came from an egg, how long did it take me to hatch?" And off she ran, believing there could not be an answer.

As I've told so many parents, I refuse to get excited about a child's growing awareness of sex and childish sex play. We can point out that to a toddler. A child's sex organs are no different than his toes or ears. "But the fact is that many parents teach a toddler to think about sex in a negative way."

If a toddler plays with his ears while we are giving him a bath, we scarcely notice it. But if this child happens to touch his penis and start playing with it, we get all excited and tell him it is a no-no, inflicting a sense of shame and guilt. Dr. Marvin Gersh says that is the adults who need the sex education, not the children. I agree.

Fortunately, the animals don't feel compelled or called upon to restrict their offspring's sexuality. Animals are smart enough to know that whatever the babies do in self-discovery is perfectly normal. To quote the master of them all on child advice, Dr. Benjamin Spock said: "Sex education starts early whether you plan it or not."

Sex, however, takes a backseat to romance in the interest of the children. They are not so interested in the mechanics of sex as they are in the simple, romantic story of how animal A meets and courts animal B.

They are simply delighted to learn about a turkey who fell in love with a pair of farmer's boots. It goes this way: A male turkey, it seems, was being raised as a pet without any of his own species around. Denied the company of his own kind, he fell in love with a pair of boots that were worn by his owner. He did his courtship dance for the boots, which were leaning in a corner against the wall. When those boots, in effect, rejected him, he started romancing every pair of shoes that came marching into the yard. Strangers who didn't understand turkey romantics were amused if they were men, and sometimes terrified if they were girls. Tom Turkey never did wise up to understand the true gist of his predicament. But then turkeys have never been awarded IQ prizes.

*   *   *

Elizabeth at eight started to be aware that there is some connection between good looks and whether a person marries.

"Beauty is in the eye of the beholder," I kept reassuring her.

Not long ago, little Liz was distressed about a maiden lady who was her grandmother's friend. "Why is she called Miss McKay? Didn't she ever marry?"

"You're right. That means she never married," I said. "But she could call herself Ms. and nobody would know whether she was married or not."

"I know she's ugly," Liz said with the harsh honesty of childhood, "that's why nobody loves her."

"Beauty is in the eye of the beholder," I repeated for the umpteenth time. "She just never found the particular person who knows she is beautiful. She may still find him. Anyway, Liz, dear, ugly is so ugly a word. It sounds mean. You don't want to be mean, do you?"

"No, just pretty and marry Robert. Is Mama the prettiest woman in New York?"

"Maybe not to the Mayor, but she is to me."

"Why not to the Mayor?"

"Because he hasn't met her."

"Is she the prettiest in the world?"

"Not to Robert Redford, but she is to me."

"Well, who cares what Robert Redford thinks?"

"I'm very proud of you. That's great loyalty," I said.

Liz let that go by. She was still interested in the basic concept of pretty. "Do you think a turtle is pretty?"

"Not to Robert Redford," I said, "but let's get out the book and take a good look at a turtle."

Elizabeth studied the turtle and made a face. "It's only pretty on its back," said Elizabeth, "not on its face. Its face looks worse than Miss McKay."

"Well, you see," I said, "according to the experts, this is a beautiful turtle because it has a lot of yellow on its face."

"Doesn't every turtle look the same?"

"Not exactly," I said. "Mr. Turtle goes marching along and checking on all the girl turtles, and if he finds a girl turtle that doesn't have a bright yellow face, he just keeps right on walking."

"That's silly," said Liz. "Can't the girl turtle change her face to yellow like the Ugly Duckling, and they live happily ever after?"

"No, darling, life isn't always that easy. The poor little turtle without the yellow face just keeps getting rejected, and she lives all alone and never has babies."

"But at least they don't hurt her," said Liz, hoping for a happy ending yet.

"No, they don't hurt her, but they don't help her," and I winked at Margy, who was looking heavenward.

Little Liz is aware that her daddy has gone to some trouble to improve his appearance by having his nose made smaller and his chin made larger through plastic surgery.

"Now," she asked, "did you make yourself pretty so that Mama would marry you like the turtle?"

"No, dear, Mama and I were already married. However, it made me feel more confident about my appearance."

I continued, explaining that every creature had a desire to be attractive. "Other animals try to adorn themselves, too. Monkeys comb each other's hair, and apes decorate and adorn their heads with leaves. Humans just go one step further as I did."

She nodded understandingly. If the apes did it, in Liz's book, that made it all right.

*   *   *

I cannot get too excited about what my little girls hear about sex from other little girls. They are not uptight about the subject, and I know that eventually it will all get straightened out. They have seen what their mother looks like nude, and a few times they have come upon me naked. After the surprise that I have an additional bit of equipment, they are taking the difference rather calmly.

While we are on the subject of male sex organs, it is amazing how much experimenting has been done to make a penis into a strong tool. Much more efficient is the insect, the whale, the walrus, and even the turtle. For that matter, the barnacle puts man to shame. The insect has an armored penis. In some cases, the whole penis is withdrawn into the male body for protection till needed. The walrus has a tremendous penis supported by a penis bone. It's so massive that Eskimos historically used these bones as clubs. The whale apparatus also can be viewed with envy or alarm, as the case may be.

The turtle, that slow old rascal, is such an effective lover that when he has hooked his penis into his mate, he takes his time and does such a thorough job of fertilizing her, that she has sperm enough to store in her body not for just the season, but for three or four years thereafter. Maybe the turtle is given a really sufficient supply the first time because who knows when a turtle will make the rounds again. Scientists are still amazed that a delayed fertilization action is possible, but in the world of the living, it seems almost anything is possible.

My favorite among strange animal courtships is the barnacle who must find a mate even though he is permanently anchored to a rock or other stationary objects. To solve this problem, the barnacle has been given such a long penis that it is sometimes mistaken for the stem of a plant with it, he reaches around until he finds a receptive female off in the distance and, thus, he makes love to a female he has never seen or been close to.

Ah love, ah life.

*   *   *

If you have ever said after sex, "I'm so happy I could die," you could be right. There's one creature that actually dies in the act of sex, the couple going out in a blaze of glory. It's the first and the last they know of sexual ecstasy.

"Who's that?" you may ask. I'm speaking of the little clam-worm. The female has grown so many eggs inside of her she is all bent out of shape. Many males are also full to bursting with sperm, and the stimulation of it has them excitedly dancing in the water as if competing at a rock marathon.

Suddenly, up from the depths comes the voluptuous female, leisurely rising straight up among them. The males make a dash for her, competing to get closest, as they continue dancing. Only one male succeeds in executing just the right kind of dance around her body, and something about his dance and his touch triggers her to such an extent that her whole body explodes in a charge of ecstasy. *Whammo*, all her eggs are released. This triggers the male so that his body explodes in almost the same moment, releasing a cascade of sperm. The eggs and the sperm sink to the body of the ocean to grow up without a mama or papa, who have died, and disappeared with their first and last hurrah.

It's hard to say what Mother Nature had in mind when she devised the various ways that animals make love. Take the rabbit. Everyone thinks a rabbit hops aboard a female rabbit like most mammals do—piggyback. But no such thing. The poor rabbit's penis points backward, so rabbits can only mate by facing away from each other. Maybe this is what nature devised to enable the gentle rabbits to watch for predators while copulating, each looking in an opposite direction.

Elizabeth was puzzled by all the quills a porcupine had, and worried that porcupines could not cuddle up and be cozy together without hurting each other. "How do porcupines make love?" she suddenly thought to ask, an unusual question for her.

"Carefully," I said.

Someday I, or her mother, will tell her how the porcupine and others make love and that she need not feel guilty about the surge of desire that will engulf her. She will understand that it engulfs us all, male and female, from the pachyderm to the penguin, from jellyfish to bats.

Someday she will know how quickly the sex act happens in some species, how slowly in others. For some tropical fish which depend on speed to escape the enemy, the whole sex act happens so fast as the male fish passes the female, the human eye cannot detect that anything has happened. It takes a slow motion camera.

Strangely enough, not all males who copulate have penises. Birds just link together as best they can, and the male sperm pours out of an opening in his body into her vagina. Waterfowl are a different matter entirely, and so impressive is the penis of a goose that the ancient Greeks swore by a mythological story that Leda, a beautiful human girl, was made pregnant by the great god Zeus who appeared to her as a swan.

But getting back to the main point, various animals puzzle even the experts. Take the panda. Since there is no penis that is noticeable, even zookeepers have made terrible mistakes, such as pairing members of the same sex, hoping to mate them. Only after they were dead did an autopsy reveal the mistake.

There is another hazard in trying to mate pandas. Like oriental potentates or a philandering husband, they quickly weary of the familiar female and will only mate with a female panda who is fresh and new to them.

With some animals, mating is very simple. For example, with the chimpanzee the act is so simple and subtle that it is hardly noticed. A female chimp in heat approaches the male who suits her fancy. In fact, a string of females, one after another, back up to him. He takes a step or two forward and they are coupled, for she has already done all the adjusting to his height and direction. They hardly move, and whenever their little communion is over, she simply moves away and places herself in the path of the next likely chimp.

That's the simple way. With others, sex does not come this easily. About the most amazing sex performance that I have come across is that of the male spider, who has to play doctor with syringes and other gadgetry to impregnate that strange, independent female. To begin with, the spider's male apparatus is located not at the back of his body, but right up under his chin and in front of his two front legs. And would you believe he has two organs? When he is not feeling sexy, he uses his sex organs like a pair of hands.

Well, sir, when a spider finds a female who shows signs of being interested in his courtship dance, he rushes off and spins a special little web and deposits a big drop of semen into the center. Then he uses the syringe tips of his feelers to suck in some of the semen. Now, armed like a doctor, he approaches the formidable female.

Fearful of her sting if she has changed her mood since he last saw her, he must court her again and gentle her down. Now he unloads one syringe into her and then, if she still likes it, he gives her the other load. If she still isn't satisfied, he rushes back and loads his guns again at the stockpile in the web, and has another go at her.

Back to the porcupine. That's another dangerous female for a fellow to have to romance. If she is not receptive, she'd just as soon shoot quills into the eager lover as look at him. She's grumpy at best and, what is worse, she has no patience.

But once the male has soothed Cleopatra Porcupine and told her in so many grunts and groans how beautiful and desirable she is, she may condescend to deactivate her quills for him. But even as he leans against her flattened-down quills, he's mighty careful, mighty careful.

*   *   *

Little Michelle at age four surprised me by wanting to know how many eggs everybody had, how many babies hatched at a time. Elizabeth wanted to know who held the world record for the greatest number of babies. It couldn't be a mother human we decided because she is lucky if she can have a baby every year. A whale has only one offspring every other year. No, we decided it wasn't mammals who were the record breakers. Nor was it feathered creatures. There were only four or five eggs hatched out by the sparrows in our backyard, and only six to eight eggs could be handled by a proud mother chicken. No, that was out. Then we discovered that the greatest number of births occur in the sea, about five or six million eggs are laid by a codfish, and 500 million are laid by the all-time winner, the oyster.

"And you know something that is very sad about the codfish and the oyster?" I asked the girls. "These mothers who win the prize never get to see a single baby hatch, the eggs just float away."

We all shook our heads. They won the record, but they lost the greatest prize, their babies.

"Daddy, I'm so glad I'm not an oyster," said Elizabeth. "What are you glad you're not?"

I didn't have to think about that for longer than a minute. "Luckily, I'm not a sea horse!" I said. I thought of that poor benighted male who is always being mistaken for a female because he hasn't much up front. But worse than that, he eventually acts like a female. The original "flasher" of the animal world, the male runs around displaying his pouch until some female lays some eggs in it. Then he's saddled with taking care of the eggs and giving birth. She leaves him holding the bag with 200 squirming babies. But then, he's asking for it.

*   *   *

About the craziest lover of the animal kingdom is the sea otter, who is good for a laugh in almost everything he does. Eskimos are said to rub noses in their courtship. The otter goes them one better. He grabs the nose of his lady love with his teeth and won't let go all the time they are mating, almost an hour.

When he has had his way with her, the poor little lady otter, feeling used and abused, slinks away to a quiet corner to nurse her poor bruised and battered nose. For days she's a marked woman, and everyone in the otter colony who sees her knows her secret. But when the little otter babies are born, she can't even remember that a swollen nose, like a human female's morning sickness, is an early sign of pregnancy.

The stickleback male is a fish who is frantic to be a parent, so much so that he engineers the whole romance and sees the eggs through to birth. A most unusual guy, with an overabundance of energy, he first builds a special nest of sticks and vegetation. Just like the human settlers of our West, when he can find nothing to plug the holes and glue it all together, he uses feces, not buffalo chips, but his own droppings.

But wait. This character, the stickleback, is only getting started in his erratic behavior. He rushes out and finds an attractive female whom he kidnaps, takes to his goofy do-it-yourself house, and keeps her hostage. What ransom does he want? Eggs. Lots of eggs. Only when she has delivered in full the coin of the realm that he is interested in letting her go.

However, once hooked on this life of crime, he cannot stop, but goes out and gets another female "victim." Again he demands ransom. She must add her eggs to the pile before he'll let her go. Finally, his passion satisfied, he stands guard over the eggs he has fertilized like the miser counting his gold. But, alas, the day comes when the precious "coins" hatch and go their way, leaving him a lonely old man.

There is a female waterbug who is very tricky in getting her mate to do all the boring work of hatching the young. First she lets the male mate with her, but instead of letting him go his merry way, she grabs him. She hangs onto him and keeps him captive while she goes about grandly laying her eggs on his back, stacking them up in rows and gluing them in place neatly. So does she let go then? No, she hangs on until the glue has done its work. So then what happens? She lets him go, and he's a defeated bug. He tries everything he can think of to get that blasted pile of eggs off his back, but it's too late. So he is doomed to walk around as a human nursery or maternity ward.

But even the bug has some pride in its appearance. Think of how he feels running around with those ragged-edged empty eggs on his back. He cannot even face his friends, so he slinks around and hides under rushes until water and time wear them off.

If I were a penguin trying to court a female, I would have to find her a present, a nice round stone. The rounder the stone, the more apt she would be to view my courtship and my funny tuxedo-clad figure with favor. This little stone, symbolic like a wedding ring, becomes one of the stones she will place in a circle to make the nest where she will lay her egg, her only egg.

You may think a stone is not a very big gift, but stones are at a very high premium in the Antarctic, and the stealing of stones from each other's nest is the big rip off in Penguin Land. It gets so bad a lady hardly dares leave her nest to catch a fish. Some oaf of a male is apt to steal her very wedding ring stone and roll it over to some other female to present it to her. What's happened to standards, the furious female seems to be demanding as she struggles to retrieve what is rightfully hers.

*   *   *

What is love? Hard to say. Animals can't seem to come to an agreement any more than humans can.

If something happens to a Goby's mate, and another Goby fish happens along, the Goby who lost his mate doesn't even notice the difference and just accepts her.

But if a truly monogamous bird loses his mate, he mopes. He doesn't wait a "respectful" few months before becoming a gay blade. He truly mopes from then on.

Love and loyalty of a different sort are also possible between man and beast. I'll never forget the story that an economics and history instructor, Jack BenRubin, told us about a little Skye terrier named Bobb who lived in Edinburgh, Scotland.

Jack, who shares our family's great concern with animals, actually saw Bobby's grave on a trip to Scotland and came back full of the subject. It seems that Bobby was devoted to a man called "Auld Jack," who was a shepherd. When Auld Jack suddenly died, Bobby accompanied him to the grave and would not leave. Although kindly people took little Bobby away time after time, and found him various homes in town and in the country, the loyal little dog faithfully returned to the place where he had last seen his old friend, as if expecting to see him again any time.

An orphanage was nearby, and the children took turns bringing him food and playing with him every day. Bobby lived fourteen years of a strange life, and, when he died, a little monument was erected for him near his owner's grave, and a little fountain was put up to cheer the children who still come to visit.

* * *

Elizabeth was much impressed that a neighbor boy, Ronald, was willing to walk five blocks in the rain to see his girl. "I would only go one block, but I would have to have an umbrella," she said. "I'll bet you didn't go so far to see Mommy."

"Oh, yes I did, Elizabeth," I said. "I went at least twenty blocks, and when we broke up, I could only stand it for two weeks. I suddenly decided I wanted to see her again. So you know what I did?"

"You telephoned her," said Elizabeth.

"Good guess," I said, "but no. I was afraid she wouldn't see me, so I got in the car and I went many miles. I found her at college and I said, 'I'm sorry, Margy, I guess I can't live without you, and this is a proposal, not a proposition.'"

"What's a proposition?" Elizabeth asked.

"It's living together without getting married." "Oh, don't animals do that? They don't get married. Doesn't God mind?"

It was a heavy question, but I did my best. "I think God understands, honey," I said. "We don't know for sure what they do because we don't understand the languages of animals, but maybe someday we'll be surprised to find out some of them get married in their own language."

"Yeah, maybe they say, 'Honk, honk, if you love me."

"Right on," I said. "We know that some animals love each other so much that they stay together for life, and if something happens to one of them, they never get another mate."

Elizabeth wants to know about how all the animals mate and are romantic. Having smelled a skunk on a car ride, she gained new liking for the skunk and forgave it for her having to hold her nose and keep the car door open on a cold stormy February day, when she learned why he was strutting down the road.

Such is the game of life that the poor male skunk has to stir out of his nice warm nest and go hunting for a lady friend in midwinter.

It's just so she can have her babies in the spring. It's certainly not that he's fond of snow, and he knows the time is rotten, but Mother Nature says to go. So out he goes, driven by instinct. Springtime birth is important to the skunk who, in order to survive, must know how to fend for itself before the next winter, even though little skunks usually spend their first winter with their mothers.

*   *   *

The day came, as it inevitably would, that Elizabeth lost a boyfriend to another girl. She had claimed to have seven boyfriends, so it shouldn't have hurt, yet it did. But soon I heard her laughing with her mother and memorizing a jingle:

"It's hard to lose a boyfriend, even if he's a dope."

"But it's worse to lose a towel when your eyes are full of soap."

"Which dope are you talking about?" I growled at Margy, sure she was harking back to the days when I was sliding in and out of her life.

"Oh, just any dope," she said mysteriously. Losing a boyfriend made him seem suddenly much more precious, and Elizabeth asked me what the animals did about it. Did any of them know how to get a boyfriend back?

We looked at a lot of books. We learned that it's harder for a human to hold a boyfriend than for almost any other animal. But we found, at least, if you are a human, you do have a chance of getting him back, losing him again, getting him back, and so on. Elizabeth felt a lot better about that. But if you were some animals, you would be even luckier. If a boy animal liked you, he liked you for life. That settled it. You didn't have to worry about it, and you can feel secure in having a life mate. From that we entered a study of who did what, who mated for life, who had lots of mates all at one time, who mated like ships that pass in the night, and never saw each other again.

Shrimp mate for life. If one doesn't have a mate yet, it just keeps burrowing along the shoreline until it runs into a romantically inclined lone shrimp of the opposite sex. Shrimp aren't particular. Once found, that's it.

So do many birds mate for life. They're famous for it.

At the other extreme, there are the selfish lovers. About the most selfish lover I have ever heard of outside the human species is the damsel fly. He is well-named, in that he is a damn selfish male, willing to sell out his mate at the sight of another flirty female.

What happens is his mate must attach her eggs to a blade of a plant underwater, so the male damsel fly hangs onto her as they mate, and she does her thing of gluing on her eggs. Then he pulls her out of the water to safety. But often enough Mr. Damsel's eye is captivated by another flitting female, and he lets go of his poor mate to pursue the new girl in town. Whether he succeeds with his new love is unknown. What is known is that his old mate drowns, though their offspring will live.

If you think that's pretty horrible, think of the romance of the praying mantis. To give that creature such a pious name shows that somebody must have had a sick sense of humor. In this case, it's the female who is some kind of fiend. As she mates with the male, she starts to eat him and simply eats him all up.

Liz had the perfect word for it, "That's gross!" when she learned about praying mantises. But then we researched and found that even here nature had a reason for this vicious behavior. The female praying mantis lays several batches of eggs, and each male she eats provides the nourishment for the eggs as they mature into babies.

*　　*　　*

About the most human romance in the animal world is that of the elephant. It starts in the springtime when the female casts an eye on a bull she likes. She first gets his attention, being in tum coy and then aggressive. She makes eyes at him, accidentally bumps into him, and keeps frisking around until he notices.

First thing you know, they're taking walks in the woods, and touching each other's trunks. He's starting to warm up a little, especially since she's getting pretty fresh, fondling him, tickling his ears, and giving him a little Swedish massage.

As the days go by, it's obvious why the female pachyderm is called the Cleopatra of the animals. Her arts are considerable, and she uses them all. She chases him, then rejects him, then chases him again, keeping the dumb bull in utter confusion. She looks deep in his eyes and touches him gently with her lips, then gives him a good poke in the rib cage.

Well, let's face it, he's hooked. He's following her around like a lovesick puppy and he's ready to surrender. She's ready to have him. She's been ready for quite a while. But it isn't that easy. The elephants have a major problem in trying to mate.

It isn't her lover's fault, it's hers. His male organs are in the usual position for a male, but hers, instead of being high under her tail as expected, are in the same position as his, down under the belly. It would seem to be an impossible project unless they make love facing each other, but animals have a natural reluctance to try love human style.

So, desperate as he is, the elephant almost sits to achieve the right position for penetration.

Being at a disadvantage in this near-sitting position, it's not surprising that the male hardly moves during the linkage. But no matter, within five minutes, his mate is well satisfied and makes happy grunty noises of ecstasy. He doesn't.

As they part, she dances around a bit, showing her happiness by trumpeting and swishing her tail. He does nothing, just eats a little to get his strength back. For a while they can't get enough of each other, and every few hours they get together again working on a more satisfactory position.

Life is beautiful, and for two or three months they are like human honeymooners. It seems that they have found perfect love. Most of the other males stay with the male herd, and the other females stay with the female herd, but the honeymooners prefer to stay together.

Then suddenly something changes, and again it's the female who instigates it. She starts turning her back on her lover, rejecting him. She gets more and more indifferent. Again the poor bull is confused, worried. She wanted him before, and now she doesn't want him. Is it something he's done?

No, it's something her hormones have done. She's very pregnant, and all her feelings are drifting toward motherhood.

A proud bull elephant does not take kindly to rejection, and soon he's back with his bachelor friends and keeping an eye out to see if some other nice young female elephant isn't taking a fancy to him. Sure enough, soon another female elephant has him aflame and confused by her unpredictable actions. He's in love again.

Oh, he'll always have a soft spot in his heart for his former love, and now and then when they meet, he will show a friendly concern, but after all, life must go on.

As I said, it's a very human love story.

At least you have to give the male elephant credit for one thing, he's loyal to one at a time.

*   *   *

Can any creature other than the amoeba-type produce young without the male-female sex act or other means of fertilization by a male? Strangely enough, the answer is yes. In nature's laboratory, the experiment has been going on for millions of years.

The creature in question is the teeny weeny plant louse called an aphid. What happens is that you have a completely female society. All the aphids lay many eggs, each of which hatches into another female that looks exactly like its mother.

How is this possible? In technical language, it is because each egg contains a double set of chromosomes. The reason that the male sperm is needed for fertilization of eggs is to supply the missing chromosomes. If human females could produce ova with forty-eight instead of the normal twenty-four chromosomes, they too could produce babies without daddies.

Thank goodness this is not about to happen because, if that day does arrive, daddies will be a thing of the past. All the offspring will be female and look exactly like their mothers, and the day of the Amazon woman will have arrived.

Now take the case of the aphids. Every now and then, probably to improve the species, the female lays an egg that hatches into a male that will ultimately mate with a female, bringing about crossbreeding. Then again for generations, all the eggs produce females until further crossbreeding is needed to strengthen the species.

Scientists have tried to copy nature and make eggs of other creatures hatch without male fertilization, sometimes with chemicals, sometimes with shaking, and sometimes by puncturing. So far they have been able to get a few frog eggs to start the cell division within the latter method. Sure enough, little tadpoles appeared, developing into frogs that looked like their mothers.

Elizabeth is too young to understand all this, but someday she will.

When she asks me about sex changes from male to female and female to male, as she is bound to do when she learns to read newspapers and already sex change has become a fact—I will be ready for that discussion. I will tell her that sex changes are commonplace among certain forms of animal life and that Mother Nature does not even lift an eyebrow.

I will tell Liz that starfish are born males and then become females, even losing the outward signs that they were ever males. So does the limpet—even to absorbing its penis and developing an ovary. So does that symbol of sexy gourmet eating, the oyster, undergoes a sex change.

Then there is still another variation. There are your everyday worms who have both male and female organs. They use them both. There is also the case of the hagfish. It has both male and female sex organs, but only one or the other becomes operative.

*   *   *

I remember when Michelle burst into the laundry room where Margy and I were doing the wash, with her big news. Down the street was a little girl whose mother told her that she had swallowed a seed that was now growing in her tummy. I smiled and commented, "Won't she be surprised when it turns into a baby?" Michelle proudly explained with her recently acquired grasp of the adult world, "I told her that a people baby comes out of a mother's pagina," Margy and I looked at each other and gave her an approving hug.

* * *

I remember when the teacher at Elizabeth's school told us with great delight how little Liz had amazed the class with a lecture on how the creatures of the wild give birth to their young.

Actually the subject had been how babies are born, but Elizabeth had gotten up to say, "I don't know much about how babies are born, but I can tell you how a raccoon and a snake and a bumblebee are born. And monkeys and elephants and chickens and fish." And she proceeded to tell them.

The subject had come up in nursery school, and the answer the teacher had been looking for was that babies came out of their mother's stomachs. Elizabeth was showing that she was much more interested in how the lower animals mate and give birth, rather than the story of plain old humans.

I remember Elizabeth's first real-life view of the reproduction process. She had found two worms stretched out on the lawn, and had come to find me and show me the miracle. At the time, I was as ignorant about love among the worms. But together we went to the library and together we learned.

For a while, worms were her favorite topic of discussion, and I must admit they are an interesting couple. Each worm is both a male and a female—the world order tries many things—and both the, male and female parts of the worm function.

I remember Liz said, "Daddy, what are they doing? Why are the worms stuck together?"

"I don't know," I said. "I think they are mating."

"What's mating?"

"Making little worms."

"Oh," she said as we watched, as little actually happened.

The love story of the worm, which we found our later, was that two worms of exactly the same size need to find each other. Even a small variation means that the openings of the two bodies would not line up. In mating, they exchange sperm. Each one has a reservoir in which to save the sperm as they can only work out their reproductive phases one step at a time.

First the female part of the worm builds a little tube in the ground, and lays eggs in it. Then she slides over the tube of eggs, and the sperm she has stored from her mate is squeezed out over the eggs. Eventually, the little egg packets hatch, and, as Liz and I learned, anyone can buy these little egg nests to place in their lawn to help improve the soil.

Elizabeth could not get over the fact that every worm is a mommy and also a daddy. "Why is a worm that way, Daddy?"

"Nature tries everything, Liz," I said. "A worm is a bisexual animal."

"Oh, I know," said Liz proudly, "bi means half and half."

"No, bi means two. Semi means half and half."

"Oh," she said disgustedly. "You're always changing it."

*   *   *

One night the big news was that a neighbor woman had just had twins.

Two babies. Elizabeth was excited. "Oh, Daddy, they have an extra baby, maybe I can buy it," she said.

"What gives you the idea they would sell it?" I asked, amazed.

"Well, they had an extra puppy, and they sold it."

"It's called the pick of the litter."

"Thanks," I said. "I learn something from you every day."

*   *   *

In a way, animals are lucky. Generally, they are raised in an atmosphere of complete acceptance. They don't have to cope with parental disapproval.

Studies on communication in families reveal that most couples find it much easier to express disapproval and negative feelings than approval and positive feelings in dealing with each other. Those who are quick to voice disapproval of their spouses are apt to follow the same pattern with their children.

Actually, both children and adults were found to yearn for words of praise and appreciation. These words of approval help everyone fight feelings of anxiety about their real worth in a crowded, busy world.

We have learned from this study, and at our house Margy and I try to remember, to find something good that the children have said or done to comment on. It's a good habit, and some of the benefit has spilled over into our own private marital life. No matter how annoyed we may feel toward each other at times, we find ways to praise each other.

*　　*　　*

The habit of really listening to what people say is a very important skill, and once can keep children and adults both out of unnecessary trouble. Half the conflicts of the world could be avoided if people didn't have to say, "But you said..." or "Why weren't you listening?."

Elizabeth and Michelle got plenty of exercise in developing their critical listening skills in a fun way. I often answer them in a slightly wrong or funny way, in order to get a response from them that will correct the message.

For example, Elizabeth is very aware of each day, fixes her calendar by her bed, and is programmed to think about her next day's schedule. When I tuck her in on a Sunday night, I may say to her, "Good night, sweetheart, sleep tight, I'll see you Wednesday."

If she catches my mistake before I get out of the room, I praise her highly and correct my statement. Children love to set adults straight now and then. Adults should let children feel that triumph. In correcting me, Liz has gained greater confidence in her own reasoning skills.

Sleepy time is ideal for this kind of interplay with children. It makes the child feel stronger, improves language skills, and gives the child something constructive to think about as he or she drifts off to sleep.

With Michelle I will often use words that sound like smaller words she knows, and wait for her response. This way I get to teach her new words, as well as check her auditory discrimination.

Once when giving her a bath one evening, while her hair was being combed and beribboned, I said, "Michelle, your tonsorial features are very striking and very becoming."

Michelle went right to the full-length mirror and looked into her mouth. "Daddy, my tonsils don't hurt. Look."

Then I told her the difference between "tonsorial" and "tonsil," and we counted the syllables and found that there were twice as many in tonsorial. Michelle will not use the word "tonsorial" in her everyday speech, but, hopefully, if she hears it sometime in the future, she will know someone is talking about hair and not about tonsils.

In a day or so, I used the word tonsorial while we were at the table. She beamed with recognition and happily explained what that meant. This way her knowledge of the word was reinforced. It's a good trick with kids on any subject that they study in school.

But sometimes home and school training get a little confused. At her nursery school, Michelle's teacher announced that everyone was going to color a bird picture, a stork standing on a rooftop with woods behind it. Michelle refused to color the picture. Asked why, Michelle said she wanted another bird.

"What's wrong with this one?" asked the teacher.

"I want a real bird," Michelle said stubbornly. "What do you mean?" asked the teacher, bewildered.

"Everybody knows the stork is not real, and does not deliver babies," said Michelle indignantly. In a moment, the teacher understood the confusion, and said, "You are right Michele that the stork does not deliver babies. But you may be surprise to learn that the Stork is actually a real bird, and acts like a real bird does.

*   *   *

We have a lot of family rules—no screaming at the table, no scooping up the rice with the fingers, no grunting.

"Unless you are an animal," corrects Liz. "Then you can go *EEEaaa EEEaaa*," and she ran around the table while beating her breast to imitate a monkey.

"No," I said, "When there is company, no animals at the table, just people."

"Well," she said, thoroughly confused, "how do people eat?"

I could hardly blame her. It does get confusing around our house.

I don't know whether Elizabeth learned it from the animals or whether she just got lucky. At any rate, a chipmunk would have envied her when Liz discovered how to hide food in her cheeks that she didn't want to eat. I showed her pictures of chipmunks doing the same thing, jaw puffed out.

A friend, Patty Nager, who works at a publishing house, became important at our house about that time because she had made friends with a real live chipmunk who lived in a hollow pipe outside her office window. Tap, tap, tap, tapped Patty with an unshelled peanut against the sill of the open window. Tap, tap, tap, and Chippie would come running.

Never did Patty have the pleasure of watching Chippie open and eat the peanut. That was what Patty was waiting to see, how a chipmunk opens and eats a peanut. But stubborn Chippie would never give her the satisfaction. It would just stuff the nuts in its cheeks until they bulged like overpacked laundry bags and scamper off to hide them. Finally, Patty wrote me a note. "My chipmunk is going to have to change houses, she has packed away so many peanuts."

"You see, Liz," I explained to her gently, "at least the chipmunk has a good excuse for loading up its cheeks. It is taking the nuts to store for later use. But when you hide food in your mouth, you're just waiting till you can throw it away where that we won't see it. You don't have to try to please us by eating something you really don't like. Mommy and Daddy won't feel hurt. So you can stop being a chipmunk."

* * *

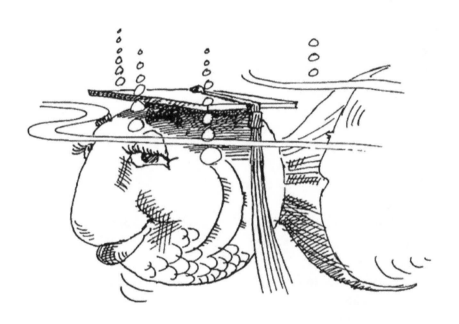

CHAPTER 7

Even a Fish Goes to School

Do lions go to school? Yes, they do.
Does a squirrel go to school? Yes.
Does a beaver go to school? Yes.
Does a fish go to school? Of course.

This is a game we play at my house, and Michelle and Liz are delighted that they are not the only creatures who must go away every day to attend school.

"But what does the mama fish have to teach her babies?" pursued Elizabeth. "All they have is water down there. What can they learn?"

There is a lot to learn down there I assured her, such as how to hide from bigger fish that would eat the little ones. For example, a *Geophagus scymnophilus* fish that lives in South America teaches her babies to fly into her mouth to hide when they see a big, dangerous fish coming, and all mother fishes teach their babies how to follow her closely so that she can warn of danger. "And she shows them how to find bits of food or little fishes smaller than they are, so that they can eat."

Little beavers fascinate Elizabeth, and she wanted to know what their school lessons were.

"A very important lesson," I assured her. "They learn how to build a house, how to build a dam, and how to do repair work. That's what they have to learn. Some people never find out how to build a house or a dam with wood. And do you know how long it takes the baby beaver to learn this?"

"I'm eight and I don't know. Does it take ten years?"

"Nope, it only takes two years for the little beaver to learn all this complicated stuff from its mother. But then you know baby beavers are very smart. They even learn to swim the first day they are born."

Who's dumb and who's smart is another exciting game at our house, and the person who comes up with new proof about how dumb or how smart some animal can be gets high marks and much attention from the others. So you can imagine how everyone looked to little Liz the day she came home with the marvelous tidbit about how dumb a bird could be—a baby eagle is so dumb its mother has to build a little fence of sticks around the nest so it won't fall out, and it takes more than four years to grow up.

Margy looked at me strangely. "Are you sure this is a patriotic thing to be teaching a child?"

"Don't worry about it," I said. "Anyway, the eagle is an interloper. Our forefathers wanted the turkey to be the nation's symbol."

"Oh, great," said Margy, "that other brainy bird that falls in love with a farmer's boots."

* * *

I strongly believe that parents and school teachers must work together to develop an educated child. It won't wash that parents have the right to expect the school to do all the educating. If the parents have not gone to the trouble of making the child curious and eager to learn before it starts school, the child starts with a terrible handicap of having no incentive.

I believe in a parent's active participation with a child in those early years of school, even if it means sitting with the little one at night to help with the homework. School can be a frightening thing when one doesn't understand what the teacher is driving at. Parents can help explain, without necessarily doing the homework for the child.

I remember how terrifying that schoolwork was in the third grade when I simply couldn't understand what that teacher in front of the blackboard was getting at. I had been considered smart in the first grade and had been put ahead, but now I was all at sea, younger than most of the other kids and ashamed to tell my parents that I didn't know.

As the end of the year approached and there was much talk of those final report cards that would be sent home by the teacher to show whether we had passed or failed, I felt a deep fear. The dreaded day arrived and I knew my mother was going to be outside the school proudly waiting for me to come out with my report card.

I looked at my card, and it was every bit as bad as I had feared. Right down the line, my grade was fifty percent. I had failed. I was a little late going out of the school to meet my mother, but when I came running out, I did the best acting job I ever did before or since. "I'm promoted, I'm promoted," I called to her even before she had spotted me. I held out my report card. Every fifty percent had been changed to 100 percent, unfortunately in red ink.

My mother looked at the red numbers written over the black numbers, looked at my hands, and immediately marched me in to see the principal. When Sister Mary Agnes, the principal of the then St. Sylvester's Elementary School which was just behind my house, saw the report card, she had to turn her face away to keep me from seeing that she was choking back the laughter.

"Let Jerry come to the convent twice a week during the summer months," she told my mother, "and I will give him all the help he needs in his work so that he can go into the next grade in the fall." She looked at me kindly and said, "I know by what he tried to do how much he really wants to succeed, even though he took a wrong shortcut."

Mother would not let her do this because it meant Sister Mary Agnes would have to give up her vacation for me. So I was left back and repeated the third grade. It was a terrible lesson.

My mother lived in a time in which the school was in complete charge of the child, but now we are in a different era. I hope that Elizabeth and Michelle will do well in school because they have arrived at school from day one with considerable preparation in speech, language, concepts about the world, and lessons in morality not taught in school. Language development, which is so important in the first few years of life, is really love development. Language development is best when it is the product of parents working cooperatively to make a child understand a new word. I remember how thrilled Michelle was at age one when she suddenly understood the word light and connected it with the light switch and the light that flashed on in the room. She squealed with delight. Margy and I were equally thrilled. We had been working diligently on that concept and many others.

In fact, whatever we did with Michelle we accompanied with the appropriate words: "Now I'm going to put Michelle in the water. Michelle likes the water. The water is wet. Now we have a nice dry towel and we are going to make Michelle all dry again."

* * *

Elizabeth finds learning much more exciting because we tie it in with the animals. For example, when she was painting a picture to take to school, I opened a whole new field.

"Not every creature could see these colors," I told Elizabeth. "You and I are so lucky that we can see that the house you were painting is purple, and the windows are green. Dogs can't see color."

"They can't?" she asked, horrified.

"No, and the calico cat down the street doesn't know it has three colors."

"Who can see color?" she asked.

"Birds can see color," I said. "People can see color and so can all the primates, which means monkeys and baboons and apes and gorillas and orangutans."

"Bulls can see color," said Elizabeth.

"No they can't," I said. "The red cape the bullfighter waves makes the bull mad because he doesn't like things waved at him, but he doesn't know it's red. It could be green."

"Who else sees color?" she said, obviously disgusted with bulls.

"Fish see color."

"I'm glad," she said half-heartedly, fast losing interest.

"And bees that hunt for honey. And butterflies and various things that fly, like flies."

She had had enough of the subject. "I think I am going to make this grass orange."

Michelle had joined the group, and then Margy, and after we had all exclaimed over Elizabeth's marvelous orange grass, Elizabeth confided that she had a new high school student in her room who helped with the reading program, but that she didn't like her the way she had liked Noreen.

Noreen, it should be explained, was a beautiful, friendly, out-going girl who competed and won the title of "Miss Staten Island."

Margy and I looked at each other, realizing that the new girl had a hard act to follow. What was wrong with the new girl, we asked, as tactfully as possible.

"Well," said Elizabeth, "the new girl didn't talk much and didn't have much to say," and she didn't like her."

Margy and I came to the defense of the girl and ventured the opinion that she was new at this job and maybe she would open up more and she would get to like her a little later after all. She was just a high school girl.

Michelle, who had been taking this all in, suddenly decided to enter the conversation and piped up with her version of what was wrong. "Well, maybe she can't open her mouth because she has no teeth. Or maybe she has braces on her teeth."

We all thought that was funny and delightful. Michelle, at four, thought of the whole experience in a very physical sense, while the rest of us were more concerned with the psychological aspects.

There was a dead silence. I admit I was stumped for an adequate reply. It was Margy who thought quickly, and with a perfectly serious expression ventured the opinion that it was possible the girl had no teeth, but more likely that she was simply nervous and didn't know what to say to the boys and girls.

I was repeating this incident to a dear friend, Helen Shepard, who commented that children always have a way of making the obvious seem new and delightful, and that it reminded her of what a five-year-old in her family said when Queen Elizabeth visited the United States and little Susie got to see her on television. The whole family was watching the queen on TV too, and Susie sat shaking her head a little as she sized up this stranger from another land. Finally, Susie turned around to the others and said, "She speaks pretty good English, doesn't she?"

The queen had gotten the Susie seal of approval.

* * *

Every day, it seemed, I had some new adventure with my children, adventures that would have been denied me had I not been home to share in the highlight of the day when the children came home from school.

One day it was Elizabeth who came bursting in with pride and said to me, "Daddy, do you want to see what I can do with my fingers?"

I said, "Yes, show me." She put her fingers together and made the letter "A." It was very impressive. She then showed me a number of letters that she was able to make—H, L, J, K.

Then she said, "Do you want to see what I can do with my middle finger?" At that point I was afraid to answer. I knew she didn't know the grown-up meaning of the middle finger, but I was still a little apprehensive because kids today come home from school and surprise you with the damndest things.

I gambled and said I wanted to see what her middle finger could do, but I didn't dare look at Margy for fear I would burst out laughing.

Elizabeth asked me to close my eyes. I did, and then she said, "Open," and there it was as big as day. She had made the letter Y with her middle finger. Now why couldn't I think of that?

* * *

Some of the choicest things Elizabeth comes up with happen at school, and I don't know about them until I hear about them some-time later from her teachers.

For example, not long ago Elizabeth announced to the class that she was going to be the smartest girl in the room.

Sister wanted to know why.

"Because my daddy is getting a set of encyclopedias," she said.

"What is a set of encyclopedias?" Sister asked her, impressed that she had actually pronounced the word right.

"I don't know yet. He doesn't get them till next week," Liz told her.

One day, Elizabeth, with her superior knowledge of animals, was advising the class on what to do if an animal swallows you. "If an elephant swallows you, you just crawl through his long trunk like a slide. But if a lion or a tiger swallows you, you have to tickle his stom-ach. And when he laughs, he opens his mouth and you jump out."

*   *   *

Parents have to realize that it is not always easy for a child to function in the highly competitive world of school, even if they are charged with confidence, like Elizabeth. I was surprised one day to hear Elizabeth, who had been very proud of her ability to learn in school, suddenly change her tune. "I'm dumb," she said.

I was just about to kid her, when I realized she had tears in her eyes.

"You feel that you are dumb today?"

"Yes. I know I'm dumb today and every day."

"I can see that you really feel that you are not smart anymore. Something must have happened."

"The teacher got mad because I didn't know the answer and she made me stand in the corner. I hate her."

"Yes, I'm sure you hate her now because it didn't sound like she liked you today."

"No, she doesn't like me anymore because I'm dumb."

"I know how you feel, and you know, maybe you could surprise your teacher."

"How?" Was there a ray of hope in her eyes?

"Maybe you could read the lesson so well tonight you will know the answer, and maybe we can do it together and make it more fun."

"Yeah," she said, "let's do it right away."

Actually, she was very anxious to please her teacher, and the next day she performed very well and came home smiling. "I was the best in the class today," she said. "I didn't have to stand in the corner."

"I know you are very happy about it. I hope your teacher was pleased." "Yes," she said, "I learned very fast." I knew enough not to overdo or pretend my daughter was the smartest little girl in the world and I'd known it all the time.

I enjoyed Haim Ginott's book, *Between Parent and Child*, reading about parents. It's important that parents learn to quickly admit they're wrong when they are, and not think that only children must apologize. One day, as I was leaving the house, I realized I was short of money and I made a beeline for Elizabeth's room and her piggy bank. Liz followed me in and caught me in the act of taking money from her bank.

Furious, Elizabeth indignantly called me a bank robber and a bad man, and all the other things she would hurl at a playmate. Margy grabbed Elizabeth and started to reprimand her for saying mean things about her daddy, but I stopped her.

"No, no," I said. "Don't you see the child is using her cognitive powers to transfer a concept from one situation into another that is very similar. This is a bank. I am robbing a bank. This is a great situation that we must now explore with her."

Even though it meant I would be a little late for an appointment, I felt it was important to follow up immediately. We three sat down and talked about what a real bank robber does, steal money at gunpoint, and what I was doing—taking or borrowing one person's money without her permission.

I could see that Elizabeth was disgustedly resigned to letting me have it back, and she started to say so, but I interrupted her.

"No, no, honey," I said, "that doesn't make it right to take money from your piggy bank. It's important to respect other people's possessions even if you gave those possessions to begin with. So I want to apologize for taking your money and now I want to ask if you can lend me two dollars until I get back. I'll be stopping at the bank on my way home."

Elizabeth beamed, happy at her importance to her daddy in his grown-up world. As Margy walked me to the car, I asked her to call and say I would be late, and then I delivered my punchline: "If my daughter understands that if I am respectful of her property, she will yield the same degree of respect for what belongs to others."

On the lighter side, the children and I had another "banking" experience.

This day I had taken the girls with me to make a bank deposit. I positioned them at the door and told them to wait for me, and to keep an eye on me. It should have been the other way around. As I finished my transaction, I turned around and could not see the two girls.

They were gone!

I panicked and ran very fast away from the teller and out the door, almost into the arms of two policemen. I sidestepped them and kept running after the children who were far ahead of me, almost hidden by the crowds.

I suddenly realized that the police were chasing me, as I was chasing the kids. They grabbed me, and one of them had a gun. I couldn't believe this was happening, and only later would it seem like a great colossal joke. "Wait a minute," I protested, "my kids are running away. I have to catch them."

"Yah, yah," said the police, hardly looking where I was frantically pointing.

They escorted me back to the bank where the bank guard assured them there had been no holdup. The cops were very apologetic, but I had no time to listen as they offered to help me round up the kids. Again I was off and running, but I didn't have far to go. Elizabeth had seen the police escorting me back into the bank, and was afraid she would never see me again. Both children were crying as they came walking toward the bank as fast as they could go through the crowds.

It was a happy reunion, one of the happiest I've ever had, and as we discussed it over ice-cream cones, we discovered we had all made a mistake. I would never suggest that they wait for me or let them leave my side in a crowded public place like a bank, and they were never to leave a building without me if we had come into it together.

"We thought you were leaving us," Elizabeth explained time and time again. "We thought you forgot about us, and Michelle said Daddy was going through the door."

I sure would like to see the fellow the girls were following. I hope he looked like Robert Redford and not what my in-laws call me—the Italian Woody Allen.

After we had all decided exactly how we would handle a similar situation if it ever happened again, we all felt a lot better.

The job of the parent is to make the child feel secure in an insecure world; to help the child cope with the unknown; to give the child responses for surprise actions of others; to help the child know that it will be able to respond to the unexpected and to have several responses ready.

For example, we have regular fire drills at our house, and the children know how to escape from the windows or doors of every room, even in the dark.

I have taught Elizabeth and Michelle not to be afraid to voice their fears. Only then can we figure out together how to handle them. The same is true of hopes. Only by voicing them can we put our heads together and try to figure out how to achieve them.

*　　*　　*

One of the greatest lessons I learned about discipline and child psychology came from a preacher, who told about the time his eldest child, Rebecca, was a little girl.

There was a mean little boy who would suddenly stop playing nicely and would pinch other kids on the arm. Rebecca would come home crying, but she would still insist on playing with the same gang of children again.

The preacher was very concerned and talked to the boy and to the boy's parents, but to no avail. One day when he was shopping, he bought Rebecca a present, but when he got home, he decided on impulse to give it to the little pincher instead. The preacher found him outside and said that he liked him and wanted to be his friend. To show his friendship, he said, "I want to give you this present that I was going to give to Rebecca. I really would like you to have it."

The stunned boy accepted the gift and, as the preacher was about to leave, the boy took his hand and promised not to pinch Rebecca or any of the other boys or girls, anymore. And he didn't.

Lecturing hadn't done it, but love had. The boy saw that he could be liked and could get attention without having to play tough.

*   *   *

People who know that I am experimenting by making the animals of the world a part of our household want to know what I do about discipline.

To answer the last question first, yes, of course animals disagree with their young. The bear cuffs its cubs if they don't march along fast enough. The mama bird tweaks its baby bird's backside if it doesn't deposit its feces on the rim of the nest exactly where it was taught to do. As for me, to establish is not to spank, rather, to be consistent in making your dissatisfaction clear when speaking to the children.

Parents who have read the various opinions on spanking voiced by the leading authorities have asked me how I feel about the subject—should little children be spanked or not spanked?

My highest authorities on this subject are the animals, however, they never prolong punishment beyond what is needed to make the unruly young one stop doing what the animal parent doesn't like. It's usually one cuff of a bear's paw or one swat from a monkey that tells the young to cut it out. Fortunately, human animals are high level thinkers and can discuss, not spank.

The primates, being our closest relatives, have a lot to teach us. They hug the young, keep them close, show them love at all times, don't swat them except to stop them, and seldom then. As for the children getting on one's nerves, the primate mama says, forget it. Tune them out when they are starting to get to you and don't take it out on them. Give them elbow room. Give them freedom to express whatever they want. You don't have to make a federal case of what we call an International Primate Conference out of it.

Since both of us are home, Margy and I both are involved in daily disciplinary problems. We do not send the child to the other parent for disciplinary action. Whichever of us is there, closest, handles it, without interference from the other parent.

Half the parents I know are afraid their children won't love them anymore if they say no to them. And I have heard children, including my own, say, "If you do 'so and so' I won't love you anymore, Daddy."

When this happens, I conceal the fact that I am human enough to have hurt feelings and I do not descend to the same childish level. I say, "I know this makes you mad and you think you won't love me anymore, but I have a reason why you can't go to the movie. Do you want to hear my reason?"

If the child says, "No!" I don't volunteer my reason. If she says, "Yes," I tell her. "You can't go to the movie today because tomorrow is a school day. But if you wait until Saturday, I will go with you."

Frankly, I'm a great believer in giving a child alternatives to soften the blow of the big "No." If you have to say, "No, you can't stay overnight with your girlfriend," why don't you add, "but you can have a friend over for a few hours and Daddy will walk her home, or you can watch your favorite show on TV, or you can read that new book Mommy got you, and I'd like to hear you read some aloud to me. Would you like that?"

If you're not in the mood for placating, you can at least soften the no with the observation that, "I know how much you want to stay with her, but I can't permit it."

If your child says you are mean, you can add that it may sound that way, but you think it is using good judgment.

In addition, it is interesting to see how the ape maintains discipline. If he is ready to move to a better feeding ground and the youngsters are happy where they are and don't want to go, all he has to do is glare at them, indicating the direction he wants them to go. Everyone falls into line.

* * *

We are teaching Elizabeth about authority and how sometimes she has it, and sometimes her parents have it, and sometimes her daddy's boss has it.

"But Daddy doesn't have a job," she said. "No, he doesn't have a steady job," explained Margy, "but he has all kinds of little jobs because he doesn't get paid while he's on paternity leave. So that means he has many bosses. Sometimes he plays music and sings with his band at weddings and parties, and the person who hired him is his boss. Some days he helps children with their speech problems at the college, and that's another boss. He has his clinical office downstairs, and different parents hire him to help their children with speech and hearing problems. There he has to try and please every parent." "Yeah, Daddy's sure got a lot of bosses, and he doesn't even have a job." Then she remembered, "I have authority, am I his boss?"

"No, Daddy is your boss."

"Are you my boss, Mommy?"

"Yes, I am. But don't feel badly because Grandpa and Nanny bossed me."

"And who bosses Grandpa and Nanny?"

"Well, they had parents too!"

* * *

One Sunday, Elizabeth was visiting my mother and father who live ten minutes away from us. They invited her to stay overnight.

Nanny, who adores both little monsters and spoils them in a nice way, told Liz to call her mother up and ask if she could stay.

My mother helped Elizabeth dial, and my wife answered the phone. Elizabeth said, "Mommy, can I stay over at Nanny's tonight?"

My wife said, "No." Elizabeth would not even wait for the reason. She got really mad. She told her mother that she wanted to talk to her father.

When I got on the phone she said to me, "I'm annoyed with your wife!"

At the time she was only four and a half and I had to suppress an urge to laugh. But this could lead to a dangerous precedence. I asked her why.

She said, "Because she will not let me sleep over with Nanny."

It was time for Dr. Dodson's famous "Feedback Technique" to come to the rescue. I told her to think for a moment what tomorrow was. She said, "School."

I told her to think about what she was going to do in school— she had been very excited because the nursery children were going to visit Radio City Music Hall. Yes, she remembered about that.

I asked her if she would be leaving early. Again she said yes.

I asked her if she wanted to rush getting dressed in the morning. I then pointed out that it would be hard for Nanny to take her to the other side of Staten Island to get her to the school bus on time.

All these facts convinced her, and on her own she suggested that maybe it would be better for her to come home that night.

I complimented her on her good thinking and suggested that she ask Nanny if she could have a rain check and stay with her another night soon.

The important point was that I had not overruled Margy's decision and had not permitted a child to play one parent against the other.

*   *   *

I am a great believer in the educational potential of television. However, it is very important for parents to be aware that TV shows their children watch during their very early years. Children do mimic what they see and are affected by crime and violence.

The most macabre illustration of this that I can think of comes from a very reliable source, Carol Kimmel, President, National Congress of PTA, who tells of this case in Parents' magazine. A little child was watching a TV show in which a character used a pillow to suffocate another character.

The child, almost in a reflex action, grabbed a pillow, too, and started suffocating its dog. The incident, which happened in suburban Chicago, says Kimmel, shows us, "in a very immediate way, that there can be a direct, causal relationship between violence seen on TV and aggressive, violent behavior in certain children." She points out that by the time the average child becomes fourteen years old, he or she will have "witnessed 11,000 TV murders-not including muggings, fights, rapes, robberies, and beatings."

She makes the comment that it would seem that a main thing TV is offering children is "training for guerilla warfare."

Speaking of guerilla warfare, it is a pity that the truly peaceful gorilla is associated with that word. The gorilla does not wage territorial wars, but becomes violent only to protect its family troop. Usually the gorilla has only to thump the ground and its chest, and bare its teeth fiercely to achieve safe passage through some other animal's territory.

*　　*　　*

We believe money is a concept that every child should know.

We talk a lot about money at our house—what it's good for, what it's not good for, how to earn it, how to save it, how to spend it. We study how the animals get along without money. They use strength. They use cleverness. The big bull gorilla, for example, runs the show. In his society, he doesn't have to buy loyalty, it's given to him out of fear and, perhaps, admiration.

Animals do save things, however, at least some of them do. A crow saves something that looks shiny and precious to him. The squirrels and their cronies save their nuts. Others save things by eating them. The bear and his kind eat enough in a short period of time to be able to sleep over several months.

To the bear, food in the tummy is as good as money.

What do I tell my kids about aspiring to be millionaires? I tell them to be *pennyaires* first. I tell them I hope they never feel so rich that they lose their ambition or interest in work. I tell them that studies of the million-dollar-lottery winners show that money alone does not bring happiness and that thirty-five of fifty winners studied had no jobs to challenge them.

To me this says that we must help our children go into fields of work that have real meaning for them so that the reward is not the money, but the job itself.

*   *   *

Liz and I sit around now and then just solving problems, the way we would do it and the way an animal might do it, to see how many ways a thing can be done. When there had been a lot of rain and our neighbors had to call in specialists to pump out the water from their basements, we lay on the floor on our backs, looking at the ceiling and imagining how all our animal friends were handling the flooding situation.

"The robin is okay because the rain goes right through the bottom," said Liz. "Aren't they all right in their nest?"

"Well, I'm sure they're all right, baby," I said. "But now I'm not sure. Are they all right because the rain drains out of the bottom of the nest. Or, are they sitting in it so that the water runs off their feathers and can't wet the nest or their eggs."

"Call the zoo, Daddy."

"No, Liz. We gave them enough trouble with our big questions. Let's see if we can find it in our book or wait till we go to the zoo next time."

"The beavers will be happy," said Liz.

"Yes," I said, "it will give them more water to dam up."

Then I suddenly remembered to tell Liz and Michelle about an insect who is remarkably smart in knowing what to do when rain floods its nest—the wasp. The wasp starts bailing out the water as soon as necessary, using its mouth as a shovel. It scoops up a bit and spits it over the side. Now that takes thinking.

I'd say it's pretty clever, too, of some termites to actually go into farming. Would you believe certain advanced strains of termites in the wilds of Africa cultivate fungus to eat? They raise it as a crop, even getting the right kind of soil for it, and carrying the grains of soil one at a time to make the proper bedding.

* * *

Ants are clever too. They have figured out how to cross a river without building a bridge. They form a ball and roll themselves across. "The ant is credited with having the largest brain for its size of any creature in the world." I flicked this one at Liz one day when I heard her telling her friends that people were the smartest animals because they had the biggest brains.

"Bigness isn't what does it," I said. "Some of the smartest people have smaller brains than some of the biggest people who might have some of the biggest brains. Have I gotten you thoroughly confused?"

"I don't know. All I want to know is whether an ant's brain is bigger than a people's brain?"

"No, honey," I said, "it isn't bigger. But it's bigger in proportion to its body size."

"Oh, skip it," said Liz making a face. "You're getting me all mixed up."

"What do you want to know?"

"I want to know," said Liz, "if the ant can do anything real smart."

"Well, it can do something I can't do. The ant can drill through solid rock without any tools, and I can't even do it with tools."

"I know," she said.

"Thanks a lot," I said. "Your confidence in me is touching."

But I had to admit the ant had me beat on just about everything but playing the guitar, and I'm not even sure about that.

* * *

The girls and I never tire of talking about what is dumb and what is smart in the animal world. Even Michelle gets a certain smug look when she hears that an animal can't do something that she can do because the animal hasn't figured it out yet. Michelle found the penguin to be even more adorable when she learned it was so dumb, it could not adapt to a new way of eating its fish.

"Ha ha," she laughed. "It's dumb."

"Yes, Michelle, baby, penguins seem to be one of your dumber creatures because the way they test their intelligence is by giving them something new to work on and see how they figure it out."

"I could figure that out," said Michelle.

"Yes, you sure could. You figure out new ways to eat things all the time, and that's the way you show you are intelligent."

What this was all about was that some king penguins had been brought to a zoo, and the keeper was having a terrible time with them because they could not grasp the new concept of reaching down and picking up their food.

It was still fish, it was what they were used to eating, but they were used to picking it out of the water as they swam. Now somebody was throwing the food on the ground for them, and they were utterly confused. The zoo keeper spent hours trying to teach the penguin how to reach down and pick the food up, showing them it was still a fish.

But the penguins would only eat the fish if it were placed in their mouths -- as if the fish had swum in.

"I know how to teach it," said Michelle. "I could do it."

"How would you do it?" I asked, surprised.

"I would teach it with a flying spoon," said Michelle.

*   *   *

One day when I stopped in at Liz's school, her teacher, Sister Mary, grinned and said, "I've been hearing something interesting about you."

I beamed, sure that little Liz had probably told the class how I had broken a record in the Guinness Book of World Records (1974 edition). "Yes," the good-natured Sister continued, "she gave a whole report to the class, and you can still see what her title was it's on the blackboard."

I looked and did a double take. There it was in livid green chalk, the greatest putdown of the century: "Daddy's a Toad."

"Daddy's a toad?" I echoed.

"Oh, don't look so downhearted, Mr. Cammarata," Sister Mary said. "Actually, she was giving you a rather high compliment. She said that you had a very fine voice when you sat like a toad in a bathtub, riding around town singing, and that by the time you had broken the Guinness record, you not only looked like a toad, but sounded like a toad. I was so impressed with Elizabeth's allusion that I gave her an "A." She was laughing. "Such a poetic child!"

I shook my head sadly. "But her choice of a toad!" I said. "She could at least have promoted me to a frog. Then I might have had a chance to turn into a prince." Now we both were laughing.

But it was indeed true that I had sat like a toad in a bathtub, riding around the city of New York with TV cameras following much of the time, until I had broken the record for continuous singing by singing seventy-five hours. The previous record had been held by Eamon McGirr of Eccles, Lancashire, England, who sang for seventy-two hours and thirty-one minutes.

I had decided to prove that in today's world there still were things that people could do to have fun and draw a little attention to themselves. As a matter of fact, I was trying to teach Elizabeth that anyone with determination can become famous and make a world record.

As I explained to her, male animals, like lions and tigers and the bull ape, gain the attention of their females and offspring by thumping their breasts or howling. That's all they need to do to show that they are supreme.

Male humans, on the other hand, have to find other ways. I had just begun my paternity leave when I decided to break the singing record. I was determined to use every minute of that leave to good advantage, to show that people can make their excitement and that such an event can be a learning experience. Little Liz had been in on every step of the planning. She had kept me company and followed suit while I strengthened my voice by vocalizing and she helped suggest songs that I could sing during the long hours I would spend on the streets of the Big Apple. We made a long list of songs and learned some new ones. She had a say in the decorating of the old-fashioned bathtub with its lion claw feet that we bought from a "Sanford and Son" kind of junkshop.

As a matter of fact, there was a little seat for Elizabeth in the bathtub, too, for the many hours she kept me company as I rode around town fully dressed and in cap and gown in the tub that sat prettily atop a flat truck like a float.

According to the rules of the record breakers, I was allowed only five minutes' rest every hour. Other than that, I had to keep singing, even as I ran to the rest room. A timekeeper had to be with me at all times to make sure I was not cheating. At first, several musicians were also on the truck, playing music as I sang, but eventually they could not stand the strain and dropped out. I also had a change of drivers, so that we kept on rolling no matter what happened.

When it was all over, I guess I was pretty bent out of shape—like a toad. But it was well worth it because my children and their children after them will have the fun of seeing my name in every library that carries the Guinness Book of World Records.

I only quoted one singing record, but actually I am listed three times in Guinness for the three times I broke singing records.

My first "singing marathon" took place at Nathan's, a famous hot-dog emporium in Times Square, Manhattan. I waited on people as I sang continuously for forty-eight numbers, with five-minute rest periods on the hour. I drank goat's milk, which was easy for me to digest, and had practically no solid food, because I was singing at the time.

For my second singing marathon, I spend seventy-five hours singing in a bathtub on the back of a pick-up truck, except for those five-minute rest periods. That time I lived on vitamin-enriched prune juice. Elizabeth, who rode around in the tub with me a great deal of the time, packed herself nice little lunches which made me drool as I sang.

My third singing marathon was, again, unique. This time I sang ninety-six hours riding around in the subways of New York, accompanied by a timekeeper and guitarist. It made a special mark in the annals of the Big Apple because, as it turned out, I was doing something grander than a New Year's Eve celebration, I was singing out the old Nixon administration and singing in President Ford. As fate would have it, President Nixon announced his resignation during my historic ninety-six-hour world record

Though my wife, Margy, has been less than thrilled about my attention-getting antics, daughter Elizabeth had caught the spirit and wholeheartedly participated in a few of what I cheerfully admit are "the crazies."

At our house, we talk of the ways animals act a little peculiar now and then, leaping about to keep from going crazy. They can act important like the peacock, strutting around with his back feathers open into a magnificent fan. We talk of all the things animals and humans do to feel important, and we have decided that if humans could feel important, and powerful another way, nobody would have to be a criminal-or want to be.

I've tried to break all kinds of records like eating the greatest number of doughnuts. But silly is fun. Silly is healthy. Silly keeps people from taking themselves too seriously, and silly stimulates the imagination and gives people a break from seriousness.

The children and I have long discussions of what makes up the human and animal world, and what they can do to improve the world when they grow up. I have already demonstrated what I can do to improve it by giving free speech lessons to New York taxi drivers.

But to return to my proclivity for breaking records, if it seems that my record-making stunts have nothing to do with my children, you are sadly mistaken. Children admire people who break records, and surprisingly, I was a hero to my own children.

I also included them in everything to the greatest extent possible, and they loved it and relished the reflected glory. But most important is that they are seeing that in this regimented world they still will have a chance to try for new targets and find out what turns them on. They need not be just sheep swept along with the flock.

* * *

CHAPTER 8

The Games Animals Play and You Should, Too

I was proud when I heard Elizabeth brag to her little playmates, "My daddy's an otter. He'll play any time."

Some animals only indulge in play when they are babies. Some play all their lives. What the neighborhood children were chattering and complaining about was that the father of one of the little playmates got angry when they tried to have some fun with him. He said playing was only for children. Or, as Elizabeth explained to them, "He's not an otter."

To Liz, that said it all. Around our house, we call anyone an otter who enjoys everything about life and plays games. An otter has fun with everything. After he has caught a fish, instead of just gobbling it up immediately, he will throw it around and play with it, catching it over and over. He romps with it till he's had his fun. He dives, and floats around playing catch.

Every farm kid has watched a cat play with a mouse, letting it think it can get away, and then springing on it again and again. It's not that the cat is trying to be cruel, but that it is having a little fun. So should you. Have fun!

Parents who have been too serious to play with their children have told me how much they regret it. From what I have seen, kids and parents who play together also stay friends, and I have noticed enough cases to have the theory that parents who play with their children raise kids who turn out pretty well.

That's a heavy thought. We don't have to make such a big deal about enjoying each other. Parents deserve to have fun. Children deserve to have fun. Why not together?

It doesn't take money to do things with your children that add up to fun. Elizabeth started it, but now both she and I collect and make up little riddles, which I maintain is a good way of stimulating a young mind to learn new words, even if the words are distorted. For example, here is one of Elizabeth's favorites which she first sprung on me:

Elizabeth: Daddy, ask me what a hummingbird's favorite food is.
Jerry: What is the favorite food of a hummingbird?
Elizabeth: Humburgers. (Raucous laughter—her own.)

We also play physical contact games. Children need to have a little rough and tumble play that gives the parent an excuse to grab and hug them once in a while. Even cats, both in the jungle and that furry ball in your favorite chair, know this about their offspring. The mother cat will amuse her baby by swishing her tail back and forth for the little one to pounce on, and the mother cat will even fling her paw across her kitten as if to hold it down in capture.

As with human children's roughhouse, this little game of cat and kitten is educational, as well as fun. The kitten is learning how to pounce on some future mouse.

I always try to make learning a fun adventure and I will say, "Let's play school," or, "Let's play (whatever it is I want my kids to learn.)"

When we are discussing what to do about a certain situation, we often act out what the various creatures would do about it. "Think cat," I will say. Or, "Think elephant." Or, "Think dolphin." Or, "Think dog." Or, "Think kangaroo." Or, "Think skunk." Or, "Think humanoid."

"Think animal," is the wakeup call on Saturday morning. It starts the family playing the game of living an animal's life. If you think this means we don't eventually straighten up the house, you are mistaken because many animals police their home territory.

The bird cleans its nest, taking out messy things to the trash heap. If we want a really great cleanup job, we think deer because the male entices his mate by preparing a very neat place for her to visit.

Primates enjoy play so much it's a pity man learned to work. They love to lounge around and be petted and fussed over. Children can tease their mothers, but they stay clear of the males who might bare their teeth and terrify them. Among themselves, the youngsters play leapfrog, follow-the-leader, and tug-of-war.

But always, when they get tired, the monkeys rush back to crawl into their mother's lap or cling to her back. Coming upon a group of gorillas cavorting around on any day of the week is like coming upon a civilized family having its annual picnic.

Of course, the gorillas have to keep on the march following the food supply and they have to spend much time picking the vegetation in order to eat it. But, I think there is a message for us there. You never hear of a gorilla dying of high blood pressure.

The comedians of the bird world are the loons. They always seem to be dreaming up some new foolishness or stunt. The red-throated loons fling themselves upside down into the water and swim that way. Loons have their own way of playing followthe-leader. They face each other and copy what the other is doing, just as people do in a playful mood.

"Swimming upside down," said Elizabeth. "I don't know what that means, but that sounds crazy." "That's the whole idea," I said. "They have fun doing things that look a little crazy. They even have a silly laugh. That's why people say, 'Crazy as a loon.'"

Some days we are tigers and we stalk prey in the backyard. Sometimes we are dolphins or whales in our big plastic backyard swimming pool, and we try to do tricks like jumping out of the water or leaping through a hula hoop. We have gained new respect for the porpoise and all the other acrobats of the sea.

Even when I want to read, or have some peace and quiet on a Saturday afternoon off to myself, I use the animals to help me. "Today I'm a growly lion," I say, "leave me alone." They do, and it takes the curse off what would otherwise be a rejection of the little ones.

Almost all the animals have fun. Elizabeth knows that and Michelle knows that. People have fun, too. Sometimes they have fun at things they do for work, and sometimes games that should be fun become work, like playing professional baseball. That is hard work—throwing the ball straight, far, cleverly, running fast, sliding and avoiding being tagged.

"You mean that a game can't be fun?" asked Liz, staggered by this new thought.

"Not if you are too serious about it. Then it's not fun anymore."

So that's why I am teaching the girls not to be too grim about their games. Play to win, yes, but don't cry about it. As a result, I sometimes worry that Liz and Michelle show signs of laziness and lack of drive to win in games with their playmates. Then I reflect on the animal kingdom and I'm glad, glad that my kids are not slavish. How would you like to be a bee, tied to one job, programmed to follow a career over which you have no control? Have you ever had the experience of studying a hive? There's not a wasted moment, with bees falling dead rather than breaking the chain of activity from feeding of the young to gathering nectar, to providing air conditioning by flapping their wings vigorously at the entrance to the hive.

It's a wonder of nature, but I wouldn't want to raise any child of mine to be a busy bee who has no time for experimentation and original thinking—no time for fun.

Termites, bees, and ants are also uptight little workers. And what do these creatures have in common? They are all a complete matriarchy, complete with caste system. The queen is the absolute ruler. All the eggs of the colony are laid by her, all activity centers on her. I find that where the female is absolute ruler, it's a humorless society. I frankly feel that other species, including humans, have a lot more fun.

I think that there is something we can learn from these creatures. Something we can learn to guard against. The termites, bees, and the ants take themselves too seriously—they are too structured, too rigid. Why? I think it is because too much power is entrusted to one individual; the queen is everything. Nobody else counts, and she becomes a victim, even a slave-of her own position. The one exciting thing she does, that seems to be fun, ends up in a game of life and death.

She flies high in the air on her maiden flight, and all the males chase her and mate with her as they catch her. It's an exhilarating moment for her, the end of the line for them.

When they get back, the sign is out: "No Men Allowed." They are refused food and admittance, and drop dead of starvation. The queen is welcomed back as the conquering heroine. She enters the hive never to engage in sex or engage in any games the rest of her life. She spends her time laying eggs, eggs, and more eggs. There are workers galore—maids and gardeners and delivery girls-to feed her, and cater to her, and take care of her babies. But it must be deadly boring to live in such a society where nobody changes places or has a chance of a different job.

I wish the bees could look in on our household and see a more fun-oriented society. Elizabeth is learning to use her imagination and be fast in coming up with a play on words. For example, we were playing a game of poker, sitting cross-legged on the carpet.

As Elizabeth sat studying her hand far too long, I said, "Liz, can you make a flush?"

She said yes, and I told her to show me. She took off in a moment I heard the toilet flushing.

I rolled on the floor in laughter and, as she ran back looking pleased with herself for having caught me off guard, I said, "Then how do you make a royal flush?"

Quick as a flash she said, "You flush the toilet in a castle!"

Should you cheat to let a little tot beat you? Of course. I let my little ones beat me at Old Maid and Fish and other card games regularly. Why not? It's important for them to feel victory. The more one succeeds, the more confident one becomes. I say, "I'll get you next time," and act real tough.

Animals in the wild playing with cubs also believe in letting the cubs win. They let the cubs catch them and pounce on them. The lion cubs chew their mother's paw or chin, and she lets them think they have achieved a grand victory.

Once it cost me three dollars for Liz to have lady-luck smile at her at roulette. It was not at Monte Carlo, but at our school bazaar. Grandfather Cammarata was dressed in a clown's costume and was in charge of the roulette wheel. He said, in an aside to me, "This child must get the thrill of winning, but I can't cheat." There was only one way to achieve the impossible. I had to bet on all the numbers, and Liz, unaware of my clandestine maneuvering, was ecstatic upon winning while all her friends were watching and the wonderful clown made a fuss over her. So well made-up was gramps that she didn't even recognize gramps.

I know children in the neighborhood whose fathers never let them win, and laugh at them because they lose. These children, I notice, say such things as, "No, I don't want to try," and "I can't." They act cautious and uncertain when I confront them and my older ones with some new game or project. On the other hand, Liz and Michelle, even when I am not around, are always willing to try something new. I hear their voices through the window, yelling, "Let me try. I can do it."

Children best reveal themselves when they play—their attitudes, their self-confidence, their interests, their sense of humor or lack of it, and their fears. Parents who want to help their children become confident and with a healthy attitude toward life, should take the time to listen to their children at play with other children, when the little ones are unaware of you.

* * *

Are my kids normal? Does an almost four-year difference in age means that little Michelle lacks confidence? Not at all. I have given her enough situations in which she won to make her feel every bit as confident and proud as Elizabeth. In fact, they are competitive.

If they have become so competitive after an indoor game that they are a little hostile to each other, I send them out to play on the "otter's slide." We call it that because the otters did it first, eons ago, learning to make mud slides on a bank and sliding down into the water for hours at a time, as at a playground.

Of course our slide doesn't look exactly like the otter's slide. It's made of metal, and originally had only a pile of sand at the bottom to fall into. But my little otters have fixed that. On hot days they put a little rubber pool of water under the slide, and splash down with glee. Climbing up and sliding down, they are soon loving sisters again.

The little girls share equally in playing with the dogs of the neighborhood. Animals are very nice. They don't say, "I won't play with you because you are too small."

*　*　*

I had just received my paternity leave, I remember, when one of Liz's girlfriends had some new hamsters, and Liz went over to inspect. She came back very sad. "I wish I could buy a pet. They only cost $3." I explained again, as I had several times before to my four-year-old, animals require a lot of upkeep, and we would just have to settle for playing with neighborhood pets. I promised, "to talk to Grandma about making a little stuffed hamster out of cloth."

About a week later, the same little friend had a new baby in her house, and, again, Liz went over to inspect. Again she came back with a long face. I wondered aloud what was wrong. "Did she like the baby?"

"Oh, yes," she said. "It's a very nice baby."

"Then the Thompsons must be very happy?"

"I guess so."

"But you don't seem happy?"

Silence. Could she be jealous? I wondered.

"What's bothering you? You have a new baby, too, you know. You have Michelle."

Now it all came tumbling out, "Yes, but Virginia," said Michelle, "was only homemade. She was not bought. They bought their baby from an agency," I replied with a sigh.

*　*　*

Animals have always been important in the minds of children in the games they play, games like run-sheep-run. In Biblical times, children played a game called hounds and jackals, which may have been a forerunner of chess and checkers. Adults also played this game, which involved a board, and two sets of five pegs—one set mounted with the carved heads of jackals and the other with the heads of dogs.

Another game played in Biblical times was, "leapfrog," played exactly as it is today. So were marbles played in those days, just as children shoot marbles today. I suppose children fought over the prettiest marbles then just as Michelle and Elizabeth do. "It's mine." "No, it's mine."

Elizabeth loves to tease Michelle. They fight over toys. They fight over being first at doing almost everything like who is going to sit next to Daddy at the dinner table.

It is good that there are games children can play, because games help them get rid of their hostilities. It is tough to have the competition of a younger sister in the family, and it's tough to have the competition of an older sister. On the battlefield of play, they find they can still be friends, as well as competitors.

* * *

Animals are amazingly inventive in the games they play to get exercise and keep life exciting. For example, wild ducks have little contests to see who can dive underwater and stay submerged the longest. In rough waters, ducks make like little canoes shooting the rapids just for fun.

Certain birds actually play catch in the air. One drops something, and the other swoops and catches it. Then he flies with it and drops it for his friend to catch again. They keep going until one misses. I guess you'd call the game, "The First Guy Who Misses Is a Dirty Bird."

Adelie penguins are very good at the game of follow-the-leader, in which they run around in single file sliding over ice or diving under ice-floes or doing whatever the leader does. When they are all exhausted, they gather in a group to relax just like the boys in the locker room.

Edward A. Armstrong, the author of a book *The Way Birds Live*, maintains that owls may look solemn, "but are really playful." He tells of a friend who kept an owl and a kestrel in a cage together. The owl would tease the kestrel by waiting until it had fallen asleep, and then giving its wing a good pinch.

The kestrel would be sharply awakened, and would wonder what happened, but the owl would be "gazing placidly upwards, looking the picture of innocence."

Playing tag is quite common among the mammals. Kittens play tag, pouncing on each other when they catch up. Deer play tag by hiding and then rushing back out to surprise the other.

Almost universal are playful wrestling matches among the young and old mammals. Kittens and puppies wrestle. So do badgers and lions and tigers and leopards. If the cubs of the cats get tired of wrestling with each other, or have no one to wrestle with, they wrestle with their mother.

Human daddies are almost unique in being gentle enough to wrestle with their offspring.

Animals who are courting become very playful, just as their human counterparts do. But lucky is the human couple, or the animal couple, who continue this playfulness after mating. The blue tit birds are among the lucky ones who never forget how to play, and they make a habit of having a little playtime before they go to bed in the evening. They cavort in the air and chase each other around. Maybe they maintain their romance so well because the female bird is coy enough to take a little rest, and get herself prettied up first to make her mate come get her, just as if they were still dating.

Personally, I hope Margy and I continue emulating our marvelous bird friends, the blue tits, until we are at least 110.

* * *

The children love to hear how I took paternity leave because I wanted to be like a bird helping its mate hatch the little eggs. They want all the stories of how birds hatch especially the oddballs among our feathered friends. They have tried them all, pretending to be every kind of bird during the Saturday morning animal games, even the kind that starts life completely enclosed in a tree hole. They need enough space in the dried mud hole, to permit the father to reach in with his bugs and worms.

Then there was the morning Elizabeth came waddling into the bedroom wearing my black coat and rolling a couple of balls ahead of her as best she could. "Saturday animal," she yelled.

Margy and I sat up in bed, groggy but game. "My goodness, what are you?" I asked.

"I won't tell until you guess, but I am making my nest of stones and I'm going to hatch my eggs on the ice." I got out of bed and, imitating her waddle, started to roll one of the balls with my feet too.

"I feel like a penguin," I said.

"You guessed, you guessed," she said. Soon Michelle and Margy were waddling along with us trying to steal our round stones, kicking them away from us and toward their own nests' locations.

According to the penguin rules of the game, we could steal from each other whenever a brooding penguin went to get food. We bemoaned the loss of the pretend stones and sat on our nests. When someone went to get food from the refrigerator, or more balls and apple and orange "stones," we ran and kicked away their stones in the direction of our own nests.

Sometimes kicking matches resulted, fortunately softened by bedroom slippers. We decided that the games of football and soccer must have been inspired by the penguins in trying to acquire enough stones to make a proper nest.

"You see, Daddy," said Elizabeth, "the penguin did it first."

* * *

Knowing that I am animal-oriented, the whole gang of small fry of the neighborhood sometimes seeks me out to play our version of twenty questions about animals. At such times, I send Elizabeth into the house for an armload of animal books, and she feels very important to be "Daughter of Animal Man."

Some of the questions are the result of misconceptions held by the children's parents. The most common question is about the elephant; are elephants afraid of mice? The answer is no, they're not. In fact, in zoos they've even been known to make friends with mice.

Neck and neck with that question is, "Do ostriches really stick their heads in the sand when something scares them?" The answer is "Certainly not." They are more apt to give a mighty kick with their powerful leg and send their enemies flying.

Other parents are very popular, and many children want to know if a panda bear is really a bear. I tell them it is a very strange animal from China, and it's hard to know to whom it's related. It seems to be more closely related to the raccoon than to the bear.

Mothers who have to go someplace for the day are very happy to let their children spend the day at our house with Elizabeth and Michelle so they can get in on the educational sessions.

The animal that children seem to be most afraid of is the snake, whether it is a harmless snake or a poisonous one. They shiver with mock fear as they ask questions about the scary snake. "Are snakes slimy, they ask?" I assure them that snakes are very dry, so dry, in fact, their skins crack and the snake slithers out of his old skin and raises a new one.

Returning to the strange panda creatures for a moment, I just went back to my research on the subject and learned that Pandas are an unusual species, so unusual that zoologists don't know if they are a bear-like member of the raccoon family, or a raccoon-like member of the bear family.

Whatever they are, they keep thousands of people entranced for hours watching them through glass at the National Zoo at Washington, D.C. They sit on their rumps and lounge luxuriously back with one foot draped over the nearest stump, as they casually pull leaves from a stalk of bamboo and eat them like licorice sticks. If anything is served in a bowl, they pick up their bowls with their paws and lick them clean. Eating like a panda at our table is not misbehaving at all, but a learning experience.

All kinds of questions are asked about the elephant and the baby elephant. I finally have all the facts memorized:

An elephant can only have a calf every two years. She carries her baby between nineteen and twenty-two months and usually has her first offspring when she is fifteen or sixteen years old.

Compared with the usual 7- to 8-pound human offspring, baby pachyderm tips the scale at 200 pounds, give or take a dozen.

Then there is the question I ask: "Does the elephant smell through the end of its long trunk?" The answer is no, they smell through their mouths—a very unusual animal.

Another one I ask is: "What is the rhinoceros' horn made of?" The smart kids come up with the answer of ivory. The right answer is hair.

This is a tough one: "What is different about the hummingbird, besides the speed of its wings?" The answer is, it can't walk.

Once a parent sent over a question to the game to stump me. It was "Does any four-footed mammal lay eggs?" I was sure the answer was no, and so were the neighborhood kids, who laughed heartily.

Turned out there was such a weirdo, the echidna. Not only does it lay eggs, but it has funny feet—the front ones face to the front, as is normal, but the back ones seem to have been put on wrong and face backward!

*   *   *

It is very comforting for my children, when they are sick in bed with a cold and temperature, to know that even cows get colds. I pretend that I am a veterinarian and I take their temperature and say, "Yes, Farmer Brown, this little heifer is running a temperature. But she will be all right soon. Just keep her nice and warm in the barn and let her eat plenty of hay."

For some reason, the children feel a little better already, and they giggle to show they may be down, but they haven't lost their sense of humor. When parents act long faced and sound gloomy because children are running a temperature, the children get frightened and think they are more seriously ill than they are.

Because I act lighthearted and make a joke of the situation, my children are less worried, and they get well much faster as a result. I hope they are not afraid to sneeze!

At our house, it's a very nice thing to have enough of a cold and fever to be forced to stay in bed. The lucky sick one gets to play all kinds of games in bed and be very artistic. For just these occasions, we save all kinds of things in a cardboard box—empty toilet paper rolls, nicely shaped stones, Christmas and birthday greeting cards, old socks, and any pretty picture or design that finds its way to our house.

When she is sick, Elizabeth likes to make sock dolls. Mother or Grandma helps her by finding pretty buttons for eyes and colored yarn to follow the mouth and nose with various embroidery stiches. Hair is also first included on by Liz, and then executed with colored yam. Sometimes a ribbon is used to tie the top of the sock head into a topknot, finished off with a bow.

Michelle does not work with needles and yam as yet, and her favorite sickbed activity is making "a painting for my room." Using blunt scissors, she cuts little shapes out of the colorful greeting cards and pictures we have saved, and pastes them in a design on a sheet of colored construction paper. Then she uses a marker to add a colorful line around each of the little shapes. The effect is sometimes very close to a stained glass window, and I have framed some of her masterpieces to hang in her room.

I know that I will get letters if I don't explain what the toilet paper rolls are all about. They are for a little girl like Michelle, age four, to be able to make a little doll head, even if she can't handle a needle and thread.

Michelle pastes little round cutouts for eyes near the top of the cardboard roll, a little circle of a nose under the eyes, and then a cutout paper mouth. These are outlined with markers or ordinary colored pens. The final touch is to glue yam for a head of hair that usually includes bangs.

Elizabeth likes to work with cutouts too. She likes to look at an animal that has been drawn by some artist in her animal books and she then cuts out shapes similar to the parts of the body. She glues them down and draws in the features.

One day when Liz was about five and sick in bed with the usual cold and fever, she was hard at work with her cutouts. I asked her what she was making. It was a bit odd, to say the least:

"I'm helping God," she said.

"Oh," I said, "how are you doing that?"

"I'm giving him an idea for a new animal," she said.

*   *   *

CHAPTER 9

Sleeping Around

Everybody's got housing problems, even the bear. Or as the little ones say at our house, "Everybody's got to sleep somewhere."

Home to an animal, as our children know, is wherever the animal sleeps, and they feel sorry for the animals who aren't lucky enough to have houses as we do, and just have to sleep around.

Such an animal is the gorilla, who has to follow its food supply and go where the vegetation is. But even the gorilla makes a little temporary nest of leaves and branches on which to sleep each night as it starts to get dark.

Elizabeth is very much impressed with the gorilla's ability to make its own bed, and will not rest easy until she is grown-up enough to go on a safari and watch a gorilla do this, or until she sees it being done on TV, whichever comes first.

The bears' problem is cold weather. They hate it. Liz had studied in school about how bears hibernate in the winter to avoid feeling cold, and how the groundhog hibernates and finally wakes up on Groundhog Day, in time to look at his shadow, and tell the world whether it's going to be an early or late spring. So she knew about hibernation, but she was able to startle the class with a new word—aestivation. She couldn't pronounce the word, who could? But she copied it on the blackboard. She then explained how, when it gets very very hot in summer, bats go to sleep, and that's the opposite of hibernation.

It's not easy to stay warm in the winter, and some naturalists believe that a big bushy tail was given to certain animals, like the squirrel, for a purpose—they use it as a little blanket. Even a little dormouse wraps up in its little tail.

No, it's certainly not necessary to lie down flat as a pancake to sleep, as some mothers seem to feel. Penguins wouldn't think of lying down. They sit down to sleep. The monkey, the gibbon, the other primates just relax in any position and drift off to sleep that way. Gorillas seem to be closest to man in wanting to get their heads down low. They assume a stretched out position.

One of the most varied things in the world is the amount of time the animals spend in sleep. A bear can zonk out for several months in the winter, while a seal sleeps only a few minutes at a time. Elephants sleep fitfully and keep waking up in the night. They put themselves back to sleep by swishing their tails in a monotonous tone like a metronome.

*   *   *

It's perfectly natural that my little ones should not want to sleep in the complete dark. Every animal has concerns about the dark, except the owl and a few others who can see in it, knowing what danger lurks.

Even among wolves, there is fear of darkness, and some young male wolves are directed to stay awake like policemen patrolling their territory while the others sleep. At the slightest scary sound, the watch-wolf howls, awakening the others who immediately join in the howling.

The wolves' psychology is that if the enemy hears a lot of howling, it will be afraid to come closer. Some say that gentle little domesticated dogs still have this instinct which has been handed down to them from some far-off wolf ancestry. If one dog howls in the night, other dogs who hear it join in. Fortunately, thieves and other people with evil intent are still afraid to tangle with a watchdog, no matter how small it is.

*   *   *

I remember when Elizabeth did not want to sleep. Now that we live with all the imaginary animals in our house, we have no trouble. The only problem Liz and Michelle have is deciding what animals they are going to sleep with each night. It is a game taken very seriously, and Margy and I cooperate as best we can.

One night, Elizabeth wanted to sleep upside down like the sloth, so all in a row we became sloths lying on our backs on the rug at the foot of the bed with our feet up, and toes hooked into the footboard. The girls giggled and talked about what the world looked like upside down. First their voices were excited as they exclaimed about how everything looked like something else—the tall lamp was a giraffe, the fat lamp was a hippopotamus, the shadows were birds flying.

I started to make up a bedtime story to calm them down, all about a sloth who was *soooo laaaazy* and lay around all day watching the hip—hip—hip—o—pot—a—mus. But all of a sudden Liz let out a whoop and said, "Wait, Daddy, do you want to hear a dirty story about the hippopotamus?" She laughed loudly at the secret she knew.

"Tell, tell, tell," screamed Michelle excitedly, and Margy surprised me by saying, "Oh, yes, let's hear this dirty story. Let's everyone get very quiet and listen to Liz." I must say she had more courage than I. "Do you know how to spell hippopotamus the dirty way?" giggled Elizabeth.

She waited until each of us had said no in turn. "A hippo sat on a pot and made a mess. And that spells hip—po—pot—a—mus."

Parents may as well get used to the fact that most children think going to the toilet is amazingly funny.

Another time we were all apes, and had to make our own little beds in a tree which happened to be individual little rugs with broom and mop handles for branches. The girls had even brought in some leaves they had gathered from the bushes to make an aromatic and more authentic primate bed. At first there was some hitting and hissing back and forth, as the little ones did not want their beds with their precious leaves and branches touched or pilfered by the other. But at last peace reigned, and, as the imaginary apes grunted at the moon and fell asleep, so did my little human apes. I carried them to bed.

*   *   *

There are various methods borrowed from the animals that would make any child sleepy. If the girls are overly excited and overly tired, we suggest that mama elephant is going to help put the babies to sleep. Then Margy and the girls and I stand in a circle with our heads hanging loosely forward. We swing our arms back and forth in front of ourselves, as we shift from leg to leg, the way the elephants do. Elephants rock themselves to sleep, and even their tails sway to the rhythm of their lullabies. Before long the girls have lulled and rocked themselves into a sleepy state and drop to their knees. Soon they are curled up on the floor ready to be led or carried to bed. End of elephant game.

Other times we all curl up together like the bears when they are hibernating. This physical contact between all of us is a drowsy, contented moment when we all feel loved and close. We talk about our many blessings, food in the tummy, a nice house for a nest, each other to share our lives with, and happy to wake us up tomorrow morning.

*   *   *

Putting a child to sleep in his bed and leaving in a minute is still deserting, no matter how you sugarcoat it with a "nighty-night" and a good-night kiss. I suspect, "No bushman mother puts her child in his own bed in a darkened room and expects him to go to sleep." And, often we treat our children worse than the animals do. Wild dogs pile up in a heap over and under each other in a most companionable way, and no puppy ever wakes up in the middle of the night feeling lost and deserted. It knows where it is.

All the primate mothers sleep with their babies against them, whether in a temporary bed of leaves they have made for the night, or perched on a limb in a treetop.

*   *   *

Doctors are learning that the amount of sleep an individual child needs varies from child to child. Parents no longer need to get uptight about it. Let children stay up in bed doing something interesting—like reading or drawing—until sleep overtakes them. Or let them do something dull, which will have the same effect.

At our house, if I want the girls to fall asleep in a hurry, for my own selfish reasons, and because a little sleep more or less won't hurt them—I play the owl game. I tell the girls to see how long they can stay awake like an owl and sleep with their eyes open.

I have a paper and pencil and tell them that I will write down the time we begin and the time each one closes her eyes, and will tell them the next day who won the owl game and what the record time was.

This is, of course, reverse psychology. Knowing that they are supposed to look at one spot on the ceiling and keep from closing their eyes, or from even blinking as much as possible, they are very sleep conscious, and actually put themselves to sleep faster, as I read to them in a soft voice.

Parents, I'm afraid, are guilty of making bedtime a traumatic experience. It should be a relaxed time when love is shown and children are made to feel safe and secure for the night. It should not be a time of irritation and anxiety with parents saying, "Hurry up and get to sleep."

Some of our most interesting conversations have taken place in those precious minutes before Elizabeth has fallen asleep. It was just before she drowsed off that she learned, for example, the true story of how the Wright brothers had become interested in flying machines and gliders when their father bought them a flying toy that was propelled by a rubber band.

And it is just before she goes to sleep that Liz sometimes remembers to tell me her best little riddles, like, "Daddy, why do rivers have floods?"

Thinking she was after a serious answer, I started to explain.

"No, no, Daddy," my drowsy one interrupted, "it's because the river gets too big for its britches."

* * *

Much of the time we spend marveling at the odd houses some animals live in. You name it, some creature is using it to make his house. The hermit crab lives in someone else's house. It finds an empty shell and moves right in.

The most far-out house is made of air, nothing but air. The paradise fish makes a house of air bubbles and hides her eggs under the bubbles. It's a pretty house to have, but think of the upkeep.

You can't tell me that bright animals are not using the houses in the same way that our pioneers did when they stood in the wilderness with nothing but a hammer and saw and said, "I'm going to build a house." Just so the tree frog must look at a tree and say, "I'm going to build a pond up in there and then I'm going to have a family."

On the face of it, this sounds pretty ridiculous. How is she going to build a pond in a tree? And if she needs water for her baby tadpoles to survive, why doesn't she go find some water?

Well, as I told Elizabeth who was listening open-mouthed to this singular story of braininess among the lower animals, this frog happens to live in South America, and I haven't had time to ask Mama Frog this question. All I know is what she does. Mama Frog finds a tree with a hole in it and then goes and "borrows" a little beeswax from a particular type of bees that do not sting. Then she cleverly lines the bottom of the tree hole with the wax until it is as waterproof as the swimming pool in our backyard. In fact, considering the trouble I've had with our swimming pool, definitely more waterproof.

Then come the rains, and, voila, instant frog pond, perfect for a nursery.

*   *   *

"Big" brains sometimes come in small packages. I think that not enough is made of the fact that tiny creatures seem to know what they are doing in making use of or adapting objects to their needs. Take the ant. Ants need warmth to heat their eggs so they will hatch.

That's their problem. How do they solve it? They solve it with solar energy. Ants know enough about solar power to figure out that if you get a little piece of board or a stone, it will store heat from the sun, and warm your eggs for you. They also know that stone or board will stay warmer longer than dirt or sand.

So what do the ants do? They build their house with a solar roof.

And to think that the humans thought they were first to build solar houses and apartment buildings!

* * *

Elizabeth is impressed with how much knowledge Mother Nature puts into creatures to help them make their homes.

"You're so right," I told her. "Mother Nature does provide a lot of knowledge. When we need to figure it out, we know how to read a book and find out."

"But a bird can't read a book, so maybe it's smarter than us," said Liz.

"I know an oriole is smarter than I am," I told her, "because it can weave its nest and it didn't have to ask anybody how to do it. Me, I'd have to read a book, and then I'm afraid I'd do a pretty sloppy job of weaving a nest to fit me, let alone to fit the oriole."

Whether the ability of birds to build houses with out instruction means that they are intelligent is a question philosophers and ornithologists argue about, I told Liz. But I told her as far as I was concerned, I admired them for their high IQ and genius for building. "They're simply great in the building trades," I said. "They're fine architects too. They have to design and build a house adapted to existing conditions.

"If that's not intelligence, what is?"

Liz didn't know, but she agreed anyway. And then I remembered about a bird who had to use its intelligence to save its life— the lyre bird. It had been building its nest very close to the ground in Australia where it lives, and it had always been safe. But then foxes were brought to Australia by the British who wanted to ride the hounds.

The foxes started gobbling up the lyre birds. But the lyres, using their brains in the same way that a human would, started building their nests up high, out of reach of the foxes.

"That's real smart," said Liz. "Who teaches the birds their songs, too?"

"That's a very interesting question, honey," I said. "Some birds are born knowing a whole song, and some will sing that song even if it's kept in a cage and never sees another bird of its kind.

"But then you have some birds who are a little sketchy in the way they sing their song, only if they are around other birds of their own kind will they get the whole thing memorized the right way. But, of course, they only need the song to tell other birds of their own kind that this territory is taken."

"Does that mean they're dumb?"

"Not at all," I retorted. "I think it shows intelligence that they can listen to something and memorize it, just the way you get an A in school for memorizing a poem."

I ventured the opinion that perhaps the smartest birds of all were like the comedians who do imitations. "The starlings imitate all kinds of other birds, and the mockingbird is so famous for it that its name is part of the English language."

In checking up on birds, the funniest thing we learned was about the bowerbirds of Australia who amuse the lumberjacks by imitating the sound of a buzz saw.

*   *   *

Liz wanted to know what kind of household we lived in, so I explained that in animal societies, as in human, there are female-oriented households, maleoriented households, and sole-proprietor or single-dwelling households and households of every variety.

And then, finally, there are joint-proprietor households where the work and authority are truly shared between the adults. The robins and other birds have that kind of household, and so do we.

Actually, any household you can think of, some animal has it too. In a big cat house, the male does nothing and lets his mate go out to work, to bring home the food and raise the kids without his active help,

If, in a typical elephant society, the female in the family is the boss, making the decisions, and even deciding when to wage war, while her mate respectfully follows her lead. When the matriarch of the herd dies, there is utter confusion until the next most important female takes over.

Male and female elephants stay somewhat together, but in separate groups. The top female's attitude toward the bull elephants is somewhat like the Hollywood producer who plays his role of star maker rather grandly and says, "Don't call me. I'll call you." The males who are the favorites of the reigning elephant queen are the royalty of the male herd.

The armadillo lives alone in his own little den, not wanting to take on responsibility. Instead, he'll go out to a party with fifteen or twenty of his friends—male and female—eat, drink, and make as merry as he can, while dragging his heavy armor around. Then it's back home alone to enjoy peace and solitude.

*   *   *

Just as some people have a summer cottage and a winter home, many animals have more than one house. The armadillo finds its protection in many homes, as many as eight or ten dens with separate tunnels. And they're not just holes in the ground. Oh, no, they're fixed up fancy with wall-to-wall carpeting of grass and a special pad of grass for a bed.

One of the armadillo's homes, a house that is particularly well-hidden, is reserved strictly for newborn babies.

The rabbit goes the armadillo one further, and uses the precaution of having two nests in which to keep its young. Some of the babies are kept in one place, and some in another, in case a predator finds one of the underground houses. Also, if Mama Rabbit notices something awry, she quickly moves her nearby babies to the other house.

Rabbits also take the precaution of having rainy-day homes and sunny-day homes because there is always the danger of dying in a flood.

*   *   *

Just as you and I want to know that a certain territory is ours, so do most of the animals. We enter my door and turn the key, and woe be to anyone who tries to sneak inside our domain. So it is with the animals.

We mark the perimeter of our territory with iron fences and brick walls. The wild stallion marks his boundary by placing his manure at regular intervals around the border, which may be several miles in length. To make sure that outsiders cannot fail to see the "markers," he sends his young male apprentices out to fill in the gaps between his droppings. In fact, these young protégés are forced to stay along the border acting as patrols. The dominant stallion does not permit young competitors too near him.

Excretia is the most common way that animals mark their territory. The rhinoceros is not as neat as the wild horse, and collects its droppings in a big heap in front of its sleeping quarters to warn others away.

Vicuna are known to be the most territorial imperialists of all, even taking advantage of natural barriers such as rivers to stake out their territory. All around the perimeter are dung heap markers, and, like the wild horses, young males police the borders.

Even the little rabbit is fierce when his territory has been invaded by some predator who isn't even looking for him. There is a story told by R. H. Smythe, a member of The Royal College of Veterinary Surgeons, about a buck rabbit who attacked a sheepdog that was running through his territory after a deer.

The poor dog did not know what had struck him when the male rabbit flung himself at him, kicking the dog with both hind feet. The rabbit's hind legs are armed with very sharp toenails, and the rabbit succeeded in making two deep gashes in the poor dog's hide. The rabbit was perfectly within his rights because his land had been trespassed upon. Had the dog lingered, it might also have felt the sharpness of the rabbit's teeth, which can also inflict great damage, said Smythe. As it was, the dog staggered and rushed on, following the deer, while the rabbit jumped down his rabbit hole to await further developments.

Dogs are noted for having taken on some of the civilized habits of humans, but they still feel within their rights in biting the finger of a postman who dares to shove even one hand through a mail slot into the dog's territory.

Elizabeth, learning all these things about the territorial imperative of animals, wanted me to show her where the territories of the cats of our neighborhood were. I had to disappoint her by saying that the cat is an exception, and does not want to be bothered with a territory. A cat likes secrecy and feels safest if an enemy doesn't know exactly where it is. To maintain its secrecy, a cat even carefully buries its droppings so that no one can sniff them out. In a way, the cat feels the whole world is its territory and does not feel compelled to stay in one place the way a rabbit does.

The gorillas and others among the primates agree with the cat and are not territory-minded. Wherever there is food and wherever the boss gorilla decides he wants to sleep is home for the night. The leader, incidentally, shows that he is different from the rest by making a separate bed for himself, laying twigs across a couple of branches or leaning his back into a little hollow of a hill so that he can see what is going on, and jump to the defense of his harem if necessary.

Not all animals who mark their territory do so with feces. Some, like the wild and tame dog, do it with urine.

The bird marks its area with song. Naturalists find that the bird is not just singing for joy in the morning, but to warn other birds within sound of its voice not to come any closer. A bird will fly at an interloper of its own kind, or sometimes even a bigger bird and peck and claw at it, driving it away.

Some of the animals who mark their territories take their boundaries very seriously. During her field research in Africa, Jane Goodall reported that during a drought, a mother hyena starved rather than lead her young out of her territory to a place of greater food supply. She would not cross over her own boundary.

Perhaps the main reason humans have done so well in surviving and changing the world, is that even though they feel the same territorial tie to a piece of land, a nest, or an abode that the other creatures do, they are able to sublimate that feeling when their brain has reasoned that this is best.

I must not give the impression that an animal will not let anybody at all enter its territory. I just mean that it has every right to decide for itself who goes there and who doesn't. For example, a male antelope will instantly fight any other male antelope who shortcuts through or stops to eat a little of his grass. But should a lovely female come sashaying along, he dances around on stiff legs to show her what a fine figure of a male he is, and invites her to tarry awhile.

If she wants to make beautiful music with him, she does. If she thinks she can do better elsewhere, she gives him a disdainful snort and hurries on into some other antelope's territory.

The law of the wild is that almost any four-footed mammal sprays his territory to let others know they don't belong there. But a badger, I think, takes the prize. He goes all the way, marking the food he has killed for future reference and even marking his lady love to show she belongs to him! In his book, it's better than a wedding ring!

*　*　*

CHAPTER 10

Are All Creatures A Part of A Greater Plan When He Made All Those Creatures

According to an African story, when God finished making all the big animals, He still had some clay left over so He made a bunch of little animals. And He still had some clay left over, so He made some tiny animals. And He still had some clay left over, so He made some big bugs.

And when He still had some clay left over, He made some littler bugs and still littler bugs and, finally, He made some teeny weeny bugs and some still teensier bugs and He said, "I'm going to sit back and rest now. You all take it from here and just work it out among yourselves."

And that's what the little insects proceeded to do.

Liz volunteered the opinion, "God did a good job when He gave the little ants on a tree a 'cow' to milk, just like He gave farmers a cow to milk."

I agreed that He certainly had, even though, of course, the "cow" that the ant milks is actually only an aphid, or plant louse, and the aphid is not really "milked" by pulling its teats the way the farmer does it, but merely by patting its back to make it release the sugary substance it gets from eating leaves.

"And, of course, it isn't really milk," I added.

Liz looked a little disgusted at all this quibbling about words. "Well, anyway," she said, "He did a good job, and I just wanted Him to know it. I wasn't talking to you."

"Oh," I said, "I'm sorry to interrupt. But I'm sure He appreciates it."

*   *   *

Each Sunday morning, the family goes to church at the United States Public Health Service Hospital, where I serve as a speech and hearing consultant several hours a week. It's a nice place to go to church because there is an intimate atmosphere. The service is private, mainly for the patients and staff.

It's not easy to go to church at the hospital. You must pass a guard who, if he sees the appropriate identification, waves you on. On this particular Sunday, Michelle suddenly became aware of the guard as he waved me on.

"Who's that big man?" she wanted to know.

"Oh," I said, pleased that she was becoming aware of the world around her, "he's very important. They have a word for him. He's called a guard."

Michelle scrunched down to take a better look at him and then turned to Margy and said with utter amazement, "Mommy, is that really what God looks like?"

After I had finished laughing, I told Margy, "I guess I had better go into speech therapy class myself."

Probably some who see Elizabeth acting so prim and proper in church these days still chuckle inwardly as they remember her outburst when she first was invited to get down on her knees.

"Why do you want me to get on my knees?" she hissed at her mother.

"To say your prayers," whispered Margaret.

"I can't pray with my clothes on," announced Elizabeth aloud.

Margaret and I exchanged looks, as she pulled a reluctant Elizabeth to her knees, still struggling. The others looked at us, some startled, some smiling. What were we running, a nudist colony? Poor Margaret was blushing as if we were. Finally, she said to Elizabeth, loud enough for the others to hear, "Pretend you have your pajamas on, dear." The dear had a fine edge that translated into expletive deleted.

*   *   *

Not long ago Elizabeth was inquiring about why she would have to start going to confession in a few years.

Margy and I explained that confession is important because it is a time when you are honest with the priest and, more importantly, with God. Liz agreed, but added, "If God knows what you did wrong and also right, why do you have to tell Him?"

She had me stumped for a minute. "Well, Liz," I said, making a quick recovery, "He knows, but He wants to know whether you remember and can feel sorry for your wrong deeds."

*   *   *

Elizabeth sees the hand of God in the gifts he has given even to the tiniest animal-like the sense of smell. One day at dinner she was wondering aloud how animals knew where to look for food. I pointed out something that I had read, that even the little housefly knows where to go for food because it can smell it almost a mile away.

Animals must be smart about such intricate things. Surely they must have help from on high to keep remembering what they must know to survive. I am thinking of the little insect called the gallfly, which lives on goldenrod. The gallfly grub must look ahead and make an opening to the outer world before it locks itself into the stem of the goldenrod to undergo metamorphosis through the winter.

If the grub has forgotten to arrange for its escape, the gallfly will die entombed in the stem because it has lost its cutting tool. Even a lowly gallfly grub must be smart to survive.

*   *   *

A lot of jokes are made about people who pretend to be so pious they supposedly can walk on water. Well, one little animal actually can walk on water, and that's no joke. The little water shrew, which is a mammal, goes walking right on top of the water, even though it is three or four inches long. It's not doing tricks like a circus performer or water skier. The secret is that it has tiny hairs on its feet that hold enough air in between them to buoy it up.

Another animal that uses air in a tricky way is the armadillo, which is able to suck in a great quantity of air until it is like an inner tube floating along on the surface or swimming long distances.

The armadillo has another good trick that my little ones admire but would not like to copy. It can walk across the bottom of a river, not having to come up for air for long periods of time. To equal this, a human would have to buy very expensive diving equipment.

When people argue about the authenticity of Bible stories, I think about the water shrew walking on the water and I think of the armadillo walking under the water and I think about many things that animals can do. In this strange world of ours, which is only beginning to be explored, who knows what can be done?

* * *

"Do the animals know about God?" Elizabeth would ask me every now and then when we talked of such things.

"It's hard to say," I would tell her, adding that they are very close to nature, closer than man, and so may know something of Him. Then I would remind her of how animals seem to respect each other and their leaders within their own group, doesn't the Bible ask, "How can ye love God if ye love not one another?" And sometimes I remind her of the manger story that unfolded in Jerusalem so long ago. "The sheep and the cattle seemed to know something, didn't they?"

Elizabeth liked that. And she also liked the story about a dog who seemed to know the moment its master had died. It howled and seemed to see something that humans couldn't see.

"Maybe when you're a grown-up lady," I said, "scientists will have found out a whole lot more about what animals can see and what they know about God."

* * *

God makes the creatures of the world depend on each other. Sometimes it's a strange relationship, as in the case of the shrimp and the gobies. The gobies are blind and they eat the bits of food that are too big for the shrimp to handle, even though the goby is no more than about three inches long, at best. The goby takes up residence in the shrimp's house and just lets the shrimp feed it.

The goby is a mean little beggar and will kill any goby of the same sex that tries to horn in on a good thing. But it is very friendly with any goby of the opposite sex. Yeah, it's a strange world down there in the shrimp homestead, part of the Maker's great global experiment.

The shrimp goes out of its way to keep the goby happy, even bringing it goodies and dropping them at its nose. And what does the goby do for the shrimp? Not much, except for one thing-it acts surly and snaps at any sea creature that tries to get into the shrimp's burrow.

* * *

Liz is always very touched when she hears of some kindness to an animal, and we have talked about a far-off country named India, where people have great reverence for life and hate to kill even a tiny bug. Liz wants to go there someday and she especially wants to visit a beautiful monument called The Sanctuary of the Ants at Shahrud, Iran, which she saw sketched in a book of Ripley's Believe It or Not!

Liz had tears in her eyes when she learned that the man who is buried there, Kasim Khan, once retraced his steps, going a thousand miles, to take an ant back to its home. It had been trapped in his clothing, and he did not want it to be separated from its relatives. All the ants who want to can live at the Sanctuary of the Ants, and no one is permitted to bother them.

Liz knows how ants feel about their families because we have sat in the grass watching them carry things home on their backs, hurrying anxiously to get there.

*   *   *

Bible stories are of great fascination to Elizabeth. She was telling the story of Noah's Ark one day at school, how a "bunch of animals" got herded into Noah's Ark and took off when the rains came.

"How did Noah decide which animals went on the Ark?" the teacher asked.

"Oh, they had to be married," explained Elizabeth. "He only took them if they came two by two."

Later, at home, Elizabeth decided it had to be the biggest ship in the world to have held a pair of what she had just learned were the largest creatures on the face of the earth—the blue whales.

It was an upsetting thought, and she wanted an explanation. "Ahem," I said. "Maybe Noah just took two little whales and the bigger kind of whale came about later through evolution." Elizabeth is well acquainted with the thought that nature experiments and that some creatures change and some don't make it at all—like the oversized dinosaurs that just slipped and sank into the misty primeval mud.

That makes her aware that man must not develop an atmosphere that he cannot handle, and she is sure when she grows up she will find a solution. She was not happy one day, however, to see a young man walking down the street carrying a briefcase, as if he were going to the office, and wearing a gas mask.

Margaret and I explained he was perhaps allergic to pollen in the air or maybe to smoke or maybe to pollution. Though we quickly turned her mind to other things, we hope she will not live in a world where no one leaves the house without wearing a similar sinister-looking device.

We hope man will stop interfering in the grand design God has for helping the creatures of the earth help each other. Liz is very interested now in how God gets creatures to help each other and to help Him do His work.

Birds are great helpers of God she has decided, because they help plant trees. In the seeds they eat are birdseed which they don't digest and which go right through their systems. The birdseed is then deposited on the ground in the bird droppings along fences where birds rest or in meadows where they hunt food.

Shrimp, incidentally, are other little creatures whom are helped through the birds. In fact, shrimp would be unable to reach suitable homes if it were not for the birds who step on the sticky shrimp eggs and unknowingly carry them to new habitats.

* * *

Why do animals go through all the trouble and grief of having young? Animals are supposed to be selfish and uncaring, so why would they starve themselves to feed their young, work like Trojans to find food, and go through the discomfort of having to stick with the project through nesting, fighting off predators, and spending endless hours in teaching them survival techniques? Why?

For the same reason we do—immortality of the species. There must be greater depth to animals than we have credited them with. Liz believes God must have given animals the same sense of pride and ambition to live on somehow into the future just like humans.

Why else would He have given salmon the drive to defy all odds and swim upstream, leaping and cutting themselves on stones, to lay their eggs in fresh water for the survival of their young?

Why else would the salmon leave its saltwater home and undergo the physical hardship of entering fresh water?

And why would the golden plover fly the immense distance from the Arctic, where it has mated, to the Antarctic, in order to lay her eggs where the days are twenty-four hours long-the proper length for her eggs to hatch?

When I saw the title of the Ethel Waters' book, *His Eye Is on the Sparrow*, I thought, yes, and on the worm and the sea horse, too. Everything has received equally His drive to stay alive.

*   *   *

Within each species, the dear Lord has placed a sense of discrimination and a demand for beauty. A male on the prowl simply will not mate with a female if she doesn't measure up to his standards. Beauty is in the eye of the beholder, and each creature seems to be looking at a different spot of the anatomy.

The turtle is looking for a certain color female head. The bird is looking for a certain carriage or posture. The fish is looking for a certain pattern of stripes and dots and other configurations. To an African lion, it's a sensuous odor about a female and the haughty swish of her tail.

I thought of the big cats when I read in the newspapers recently about a woman who had started a new club for women only called "Man Watchers." Suzy Mallery, who founded the club that now has 4,000 members, reports that "More women watch the buttocks of men than any other area."

In comparison, according to Playboy magazine, men make first judgment by looking at a woman's bosom.

There is such a variety in the types of human women that somewhere in the world almost any part of the anatomy has been idealized. In one primitive tribe, the true mark of beauty in a woman is a gigantic buttocks. If she is so large behind that she has to be helped up, she is indeed a beauty queen.

Just as ludicrous is the drive for huge mammary glands as a sign of beauty, a drive so intense that thousands of women spend millions of dollars to undergo silicone implantations.

So you see, we're still not too far removed from the lower animals to want to have bovine breasts and buttocks like giant sponges of the deep.

Mankind has never needed to take lessons in vanity from the animals. In fact, man has always sought to add the beauty of the bird and the beast to his own, even wiping out whole species of birds to serve as his decorations.

But the ultimate decoration I read about was current in the 1700s, when people of high fashion shaved off their eyebrows and glued on fancy eyebrows made of mouse fur.

Liz's first reaction on hearing that was to say, "Oh, good, maybe that's the way to get rid of all the mice in people's houses." But for herself, no thank you. Animal is still animal, and she will not wear it.

So mouse eyebrows are out, no matter what fashions are revived.

*   *   *

Are animals vain? They seem to be every bit as vain as humans, and if they knew how to invent cosmetics, I have a feeling they would apply them liberally. As it is, the monkey family decorate themselves with leaves and flowers.

The female otter spends endless time fluffing her fur, and her mate does almost as much grooming. True, the otter must get rid of the water in its fur, but the grooming goes beyond sheer necessity.

Beavers, too, spend a lot of time prettying up, and the female beaver and young males are much more concerned with their appearance and spend more time on it than an old codger who's seen better days. As soon as she enters the beaver den, mama beaver starts combing her fur, using a special nail on her paw for up to a half hour.

Birds preen and are very particular about how their feathers look. Even bugs can be meticulous about cleaning and polishing themselves by rubbing until they achieve a high shine.

Monkeys spend endless hours grooming each other, and experts now believe they are not just picking off any little lice or fleas that may be present, but are using the search for insects as an excuse to be petting and prettying each other.

Elizabeth has raised a question that I have not seen answered anywhere in my reading on animals, but which has profound ramifications. I hope that scientists will someday address themselves to answering her question: How does an animal know what kind of animal it is if it doesn't have a mirror to look in and see what it looks like?

To me that seems a very profound question. It's kind of scary. Did God make creatures so vain that their own kind look most beautiful in all the world, and so they recognize their own kind by this computerized input?

Some creatures, of course, do see their own image and either fall in love with it or become furious at the supposed competitor. I once knew a crow who would spy its mirror image in the windowpane of a mountain lodge every morning and would attack the pane of glass furiously, until it finally broke the window. It probably figured its arch enemy had been frightened away, at least until the window was replaced with a sturdier one.

The intimation here is that to a snout-nosed, beady-eyed, short-legged, fat-blimp-bodied, rough, wrinkle-skinned, mud-covered hippopotamus, people are ugly and hippopotami are beautiful.

In addition, I have come to the conclusion that, if people want to think more deeply about themselves and mankind and its condition, they must study the animals.

I think the greatest lesson for kids about the criteria for beauty among the individual animals of the world is contained in a little storybook for children aged four to eight that was published by Parents' Magazine Press. The name of the book is *Monkey Face*, and in it Frank Asch tells a wonderful story about a little monkey who is on his way home from school with a picture he has just drawn of his mother.

He's happy because he's going to give it to his mother for a present. But each time he meets a different animal friend, they tell him how he can make that picture more beautiful according to each one's idea of beauty, and each time a suggestion is made, the monkey has to change his drawing. For example, the elephant thought the monkey's picture of his mother would be much prettier if she had a big long nose down to the ground.

Then the owl thought the monkey would be beautiful if only she had big round eyes. The rabbit suggested that the real mark of beauty was big long ears.

By the time the poor little monkey got home, he had a composite picture that one could gag over. Only a mother could love such a present and his mommy proved herself a loving mother by exclaiming over it.

But the little fellow had learned his lesson: monkey face is beautiful.

* * *

There was a time when Elizabeth wanted to be a nurse. She wrapped me in endless bandages. "Elizabeth," I said, to pass the time, "what would you do if this were for real and I came to you all bloodied up?"

"I'd cry," she said, starting to cry already.

"Well," I said, "you've got to learn to be tough."

"The animals are tough. When they are hurt, they try to take care of themselves." And I told her gently how a fox saved its life by gnawing off its own leg when it was caught in a fur trader's cruel trap. It was the only way it could escape.

"Did it live?"

"Yes, it did, and it got married even with three legs and had puppies."

"Did they have three legs?"

"No," I said, "they didn't. They had four legs, but they thought she looked beautiful with three legs because she was their mommy."

CHAPTER 11

What Kind of Parent Are You Compared With, Say, a Hyena, An Alligator, or a Bunny Rabbit?

For years now everybody has been singing the praises of motherhood. Come on now, let's hear it for all the mothers of the world.

You are proud, perhaps, about what good care you took of your baby, getting up three times every night to see that it was covered and warm?

Let me tell you something. The mother rabbit, much maligned as a scatterbrain and bearing the reputation of a nymphomaniac, is one of the most stable and dedicated mothers of the world, pulling fur out of her own body to keep her babies warm.

One of the most touching stories of a mother's self-sacrifice is that of the octopus off the shores of Southern California. She starves herself for more than three months, while she spends all her time giving individual attention to all her eggs, which she has attached to a rock at the end of little strings—one egg per string.

Why can't she just let them lie there and go find a good lunch to keep her strength up? For two reasons. For one thing, too many creatures find octopus eggs a delicacy, and she is busy fighting off these predators. But even more important, the eggs are prone to fungus infections that would prevent the babies' birth. So the poor octopus must keep churning away with all eight arms, cleaning her eggs and spraying them and forcing air to come between them.

And have you heard about the salamander? That loving mama curls her little body around her eggs while they are hatching and does not have a bit of food until they are hatched. She's afraid, you see, that someone will eat the eggs if she goes away for an instant. The father is long since gone, never thinking he might have a hungry mate back there somewhere.

Some creatures must help their young escape from the egg—the alligator is one of those mothers. It actually must crack the caked mud around the egg. If she didn't hear her young one cry for help as it tries to get out, it would die. But she's there, and she rushes to it with maternal concern.

Animals don't have to take a backseat to anyone in displaying parent love. A lemur monkey loves its offspring so much that if its baby dies, it can't accept it, and it continues to carry it around for a long, long time.

*   *   *

We were having a game of who would you want to be if you were an animal and someone was attacking your mother. "Who would you want to have protect you?" I asked.

"A tiger," yelled Michelle first, sure that she had chosen the fiercest animal.

"No," said Liz, remembering something she had learned. "A big bull can just pick up a tiger on his horn and throw it over his shoulder."

"You're right, Liz," I said. "That was a very smart answer. But there is just one problem. You are right if they are fighting fair, one-to-one combat. But if there is a gang of tigers attacking the bull or cow at one time, then Michelle is right, the tigers win."

Now it was Michelle's turn to beam. "What animal do you want to be, Daddy?"

"Well, Michelle, if I were the baby, I think maybe I'd want my mama to be a hyena because you know what? The hyena has the strongest jaws in the animal kingdom, and if she gets ahold of you, wow!"

Then we switched and tried to decide what animal we'd choose to have the nicest, gentlest mommy.

"I want a mommy that doesn't get angry," said Michelle. "My mommy gets angry."

"Yes," I said, "but not too hard, and don't you think she's right when she does and you have been naughty? And she's only human, you know and that means getting angry once in a while."

"Yeah, she's only human," Michelle agreed, "but when I grow up I will never, never get angry at my babies."

"Fine," I said. "That means you are going to have perfect babies and you are going to be the perfect mama and never get upset with your baby."

"Yes," she said.

"So what kind of an animal baby are you going to be?" Liz asked, anxious to get on with the game. "I'll take my tum first. I'm going to be a baby otter and ride around on a seaweed raft all day, and play in the water. And my mama will play with me all day." Michelle said, "I'm going to be a baby kangaroo and stay in my mama's pouch and peep out at everything, and my mama will protect me. "What will she do to protect you?"

"She'll give a karate chop." Michelle demonstrated a kangaroo protecting its young.

"Don't forget a good swift kick," I said, imitating, I hoped, a kangaroo using her best weapon.

* * *

Everywhere in nature, with some notable exceptions, you see sterling examples of motherhood. Right in your own backyard you have probably seen a mother bird going through her "broken wing" act, pretending to have a broken wing to distract a predator from seeing where her baby birds are hidden.

Sometimes she loses her life in this dangerous ploy. In that case, the young ones may die anyway, unless there is a father bird to keep bringing home the endless supply of food.

In her desperation, the mother is saying, "Here, eat me, I am defenseless. Leave my child alone."

*   *   *

Now that the mothers of the wild have taken a deep bow, let's hear it for the fathers of nature's wonderland.

There is no doubt about it, generally the mothers of the world have an instinct that leads them to do drastic things. But, in some cases, fathers and mothers share the same madness. The mating gulls, for example, tear the soft feathers from their breasts to make a warm nest lining for their babies, even before the eggs are laid.

You want to hear about a real role reversal? Take a look at the emu. This is no dainty little bird-it's the big shot, the largest bird in Australia and next in size to the ostrich, the largest bird in the world.

So we're talking about a rather important personage. But on a scale of one to ten, this bird rates ten on being confused. What I am trying to say is that the emu has an identity crisis and needs a psychiatrist right away.

To anyone who wants to see parenthood a fifty-fifty basis, I direct them to the emu.

The male emu sits on the eggs not just for a few days or sporadically as his mate needs food. No, the emu hatches them all by himself, sitting on them the full fifty-eight to sixty-one days—the entire months.

The male emu then feeds and protects and is the sole "parent" of the little ones, nurturing them and hustling to bring them insects. He teaches them to eat a balanced diet of fresh vegetables and fruit with their protein.

The emu stays with the little ones not just during their babyhood while he is dropping food in their mouths, but for eighteen long months.

Finally, sometime before their second birthday, the emus leave home, and dad catches his breath and wonders what it's all about. From start to finish, he has been the full provider. His mate has only contributed the eggs. And, come to think of it, he didn't even get to pick her-she picked him!

If you think the emu odd, consider the ostrich. The male gets himself into an impossible situation where he, too, is taken advantage of. What happens is that when the male shows he is in the mood to be friendly, a whole bunch of females lay eggs and go sashaying off to party, leaving him to take care of them. Sometimes there are fifty to one hundred eggs to care for, and there he is doing the job alone for six weeks or more. But proof that he really enjoys his fatherhood is that if another male ostrich came along and wanted to help, the big daddy would tell him to get lost, with a swift kick.

And talk about taking advantage of a goodhearted guy, let me tell you about a kind of dumb henpecked toad humorously referred to as the obstetric toad. His wily mate hatches her eggs in strings and, to get rid of them, she simply winds them around her mate's hind legs and lets *him* worry about them. He has to drag them around, until they hatch. Needless to say, he's not the most popular man at a party until he gets rid of his load. But his mate is the life of the party, no conscience.

Elizabeth and her friend Roxanna had listened to this story and were not pleased with the mean old lady toad. "Why did he let her do it?" Roxanna asked. I had to explain that the poor cluck of a toad was obviously not as smart as his mate and didn't know what she was doing until he was trapped.

*   *   *

Males are not the most honored people around the newborn baby, even among the animals. Sometimes males just take the hint and stay away, and at other times they are just driven out. Such is the case with the beavers.

The female beaver actually drives off her mate, as well as her adolescent children, after she gets pregnant a second time and is ready to give birth to a new litter. Young beavers, like their human counterparts, sometimes cling to their parents and hate to give up their life of dependency.

Mother birds actually shove their young ones out of the nest before the first season is over. But the beaver mother lets her young ones stay until they are almost two years old. Since she is pregnant with her new litter, she is faced with having two sets of young ones around the beaver lodge at the same time.

In her heightened nervous condition, this is almost too much for her to bear. She starts cleaning house, throwing out all her children, and when her eye falls on him, their father as well.

Usually her mate comes slinking back, after he's made sure that the youngsters are well on their way to building a beaver lodge of their own, and will never darken her doorway again. But the irritable beaver mother is taking the risk when she drives her mate out that he may not return. Sometimes he finds greener pastures and bluer water elsewhere.

*   *   *

Let's face it. Not everybody's perfect.

A lot of human males are rotten fathers in the same way that the panda is. The panda father stays away, and in fact, keeps his own house in a hollow tree or cave. He has no interest in his lonely offspring, and the mother panda must play with the baby and keep it company. Daddy could care less. He acts like an only child who has not been trained to play with other children and share. And that's certainly the truth. Every panda is an only child.

A much overrated male is the lion, the king of the jungle. It takes a real emergency to make that fellow move. Most of the time, he's reclining on his royal rear, watching the women of his harem work.

It's not the male lion who goes stalking a dangerous animal for food. No, indeed, it's the harem of females who, being smaller and weaker, going hunting together.

Once the team has dragged home the dead animal, the king of the jungle jumps up and finally goes into action, not to congratulate them with appreciative grunts, but with a terrible roar that says, "Step aside!" Then he proceeds to eat his fill, like a big bully, keeping away the cubs and lionesses until he's satisfied.

In contrast to his swaggering, the lioness is such a nice lady that if she is producing milk, she will permit any little lion cub to have a drink.

A more timid father is the sea otter. When danger comes, he and his mate embrace and hang onto each other for dear life until the danger is over or they are dead. They look so human it hurts. The best defense of the otter is speed. They can reverse direction like a flying saucer, and hunters have found that otters can even duck out of the way of a flying bullet if they see it coming. If so, their reflex actions and nervous systems are better than those of humans.

By way of poor male providers, I rate the lark high. While most male birds work diligently to provide a little nourishment for their mates, bringing it to them while they sit on the nest, this guy can't be bothered.

He lets his mate get her own food, and keeps rushing madly back to the nest to make sure that the eggs are still warm. It makes me wonder where they got that expression, "Happy as a lark." It surely must refer to the male.

* * *

The hard truth is that few animals indulge in sentimentality as we do. They know by instinct that the weak will fall sooner or later, and they make it sooner. Even our favorite friend, the domesticated dog, will turn its back on a sick puppy.

The wild dogs are among the few that nurture their sick and feed it regurgitated food. That kindness was probably bred out of them when they mated with other animals, possibly wolves, to become the forebears of the dog in our living room.

Wild dogs rate among the best parents of the animal kingdom. Usually, adult animals like lions and tigers grab their food before letting the juvenile members of the pack have any. But wild dogs are different. They actually stand guard, and let the younger members eat all they want before digging in for their share. Waterfowl make some kind of tough mamas.

When mama thinks it's time to teach the babies to swim, she deserts those who can't make it and leads the strong ones to water. The others may perish. She may never return to the nest on the shore to see what happened to the weaker ones.

*   *   *

Every child, it seems, eventually worries that he or she has been given to the wrong parents, and Elizabeth was no exception. Even reassurance that a doctor and nurse had immediately put a little bracelet on her wrist to tell her whom she belonged, failed to convince her for a time.

Surely the animals are way ahead of us in being able to recognize their own, even in a sea of infants.

When Liz worried about her parentage, it helped to discuss how various animals of the world recognize their young, while others just don't care. Having launched them, they take no further notice.

"Elizabeth," I said, "just be glad you're a mammal. Parents take much better care of their kids. Some creatures like oysters and certain fish just let their eggs drift away, and don't even wait till they're hatched. So if they meet again, they don't even know if they're related."

Urged on by Liz, we made many forays into the library and to the zoo to read and talk to experts about the wonderful ways in which animals know their young.

A mother bear recognizes its young by the smell, and so do the young recognize their mother by her smell.

A mother goat recognizes its baby by the taste and odor of its fur, and if it is not permitted to lick its newborn kid for an hour or two after birth, it will forget and will not recognize the baby at all. It will even let it die, rather than let it nurse.

"You mean the baby goat dies?" asked Elizabeth with great concern.

"No, not if it's a goat in a barnyard. How the farmers solve the problem is that they let another new mother lick the rejected baby goat at the same time she is licking her own kid, and soon she is feeding both babies."

But Elizabeth was not to be satisfied that easily. "What if there isn't any other new mama goat? Then does it die?"

"No, baby," I assured her. "Because, you see, a farmer is smarter than a goat. The mother goat has a lot of milk in its bag, and the baby goat needs the milk. So the farmer milks the goat and puts the milk in a bottle, just like your baby bottle, and he feeds the goat that way."

"It's not the same for the baby," she said, still not happy. "The mama still should feed her." Elizabeth was so saddened by this news about goats that I quickly told her about the kindly mother moose who will adopt any baby moose that has wandered away from its own mother, or whose mother has died.

Elizabeth decided she would adopt many babies, and I complimented her for demonstrating that a human mother is one of those nice creatures who can love a baby that is not her own.

But the human mother is not the only one who can enjoy someone else's babies and try to look after them. A mother monkey will allow other female monkeys to pick up and cuddle her baby.

* * *

"Did you know me when I was born?" Elizabeth wanted to know.

"No," I had to admit. "Mama and I were not as smart as the animals. Not till we hugged you and got acquainted with you did we recognize you out of all those babies at the hospital. But then, once I got acquainted with that little face, I'd have known you anywhere."

"I wish they hadn't washed me when I was born, so my mother could recognize me by how I smell," Liz ventured. I told her that perhaps it was something else that made mothers recognize their own babies. I told her that baby bats, scientists have found, get used to their mother's voice even before they are born. Even though there are hundreds of bats in a barn, the mother and newborn baby always find each other, guided by sound, sometimes ultrasonic sound.

Elizabeth liked that and she liked learning that a mother duck talks to the eggs while she is sitting on them before they start to hatch. Mother and ducklings are well acquainted when the fuzzy little babies come pecking their way out of the eggs. But then little Liz got an attack of the giggles as she learned that a baby goose will follow any moving object she sees first, and think that it is mother, if you take away its real mother as the eggs are hatching.

"That's dumb!" she said.

"Yes, dumb is dumb. But people get tricked too."

"But animals aren't dumb, are they, Daddy? They know inside what to do."

"Well, they know a lot, darling, but dumb is dumb everywhere in the world. People are dumb about some things and smart about others. You can give a chicken a fake egg, and it sits on it and tries to hatch it and doesn't know the difference, and that may be good because it makes the hen feel better and it gives it hope to be sitting on anything that looks like an egg."

"You can take a penguin and give it a stone instead of an egg, and it will sit on it and try to hatch it. Yes, you can. And you can take a baby monkey and give it a terry cloth towel stuffed with cotton, and it will think that's its mother. You can put a nipple on one side of the towel, and the baby monkey will cling to it and go to it for comfort and protection."

"Ha ha," said Liz, with eight-year-old assurance. "That's a dumb monkey because everybody knows there are supposed to be two nipples or four nipples on every animal."

"Aha, I gotcha," I said, pouncing on Liz and throwing her in the air. "Don't you remember all the puppies and the kittens and those nipples in two rows under their mama?"

Then I told her the thing that delighted her the most about how the creatures of the wild feed their young—the feeding of the baby whale. She wouldn't believe it, so we went to the library and talked to someone at the zoo, and sure enough, it was true.

The mama whale has a terrible time feeding her young. She's in the ocean, but she has two nipples just like an orangutan or like mommy because she is a mammal, too. The whale has to feed her baby without drowning it, and she needs air for herself. She turns over on her back and sticks up one nipple for the baby whale to grasp. When it has drunk from that one, she changes her position and exposes a second nipple.

"But the strangest part of it," I told Liz, "is that the baby does not suck the nipple. The poor mama whale has to exert pressure to squirt the milk into the baby's mouth."

That, Liz decided, was the cutest.

*   *   *

One of the problems everybody shares is the fear of being left behind. A child doesn't want to be deserted, neither does the monkey's. The baby monkey clings to its mother's fur with its very life, so it won't be deserted. Psychologists tell us that the first fear the newborn human baby faces is that of abandonment. Part of the early screaming of the newborn baby is probably simply the need for some reassurance that it has not been abandoned.

No self-respecting monkey, rat, or kangaroo would treat its offspring the way some humans treat theirs. The mother monkey hangs onto that baby at all times, and lets it know she's there. The kangaroo mama only tosses its baby out of the pouch in an extreme emergency—to save it from predators.

In contrast, think of the poor human baby who is left alone in his crib or playpen for hours at a time. To busy parents, time seems to fly, but to an infant with nothing to do but watch, listen, and worry about whether anyone will come, every minute stretches into an eternity.

Among the humane mothers have been the Indian squaws who strapped their babies to their backs and took them along wherever they went, wearing them like the most beautiful jewel. Whenever I see a modem parent following the Indian custom, even when zipping along on a bicycle, I applaud mentally.

*   *   *

It is very important that human fathers get into the act as quickly as possible after the new baby's birth. Don't take my word for

172

it. It is the finding of scientists that a baby can develop a bond with its father in the first three days after birth.

Doctors maintain that this engagement develops at that early stage, the child gets an increased sense of self-esteem that will help its growth into a confident trouble-free child.

I developed this theory with Michelle, and I believe it is true because she has a fine sense of self-esteem and seems relatively trouble free at age four.

But all kinds of pressures lie ahead for our girls. They will be tempted by their friends to try drugs, perhaps at an early age. I hope when that happens, they will talk to me about it in the same way they come to me now with their little problems.

But long before they are tempted, I will have prepared them for the problem of drugs in a casual way. I will tell them that this thing might happen and that some of their friends will put a lot of pressure on them to give drugs a try. "They are going to tell you it's a lot of fun and exciting, and that you're a scaredy cat if you don't. Do not believe them."

These friends might be stubborn. I know they can be, but say no. I will tell you and them that drugs are not smart and that people that fool with them are not smart, but dumb.

They will ask me why, and I will tell provide for them to see with their own eyes what doctors say happen to children who get on drugs, how they cannot get along without them once they start, and how they become the slave of those who can supply them. Life will be full of problems.

I have started their drug education by reading aloud several articles about babies who were born to addicted. Liz was greatly distressed to hear how the babies had suffered withdrawal pains, and had been in such agony that small amounts of drugs were administered so that the baby could gradually get healthy.

"That mommy made a terrible mistake," said Liz. "I'm going to be a mommy like my mommy. "I agree, that would be a wonderful," I said.

*   *   *

If you think it's tough to be a human mother of a big family, think of this. At least you have the little characters one at a time. Twins and triplets are rarer. The armadillo always has quadruplets. Quintuplets are not uncommon in the animal world, not even for your friendly dog or cat.

Fish have hundreds of offspring swimming after them, and an octopus may have as many as 40,000 little bundles of joy.

If giving birth to a seven-pound object is not easy, consider the kiwi. That poor mama has to discharge a giant egg that is one-third her weight. And no doctor stands by to help her to put to sleep or tranquilize her. In comparison, to equal the kiwi feat, the average human mother would have to give birth to a forty or forty-five-pound baby. *Ouch!*

*   *   *

Liz thought all animals carried their young by the scruff of the neck, as she had seen the dogs and cats in our neighborhood do. One of her greatest thrills was finding out how inventive the clever animal mothers are in finding ways to carry their babies, considering they have no hands.

Even monkey family mothers who do have hands don't necessarily carry their babies the way Margy carried Michelle. The mother gibbon, for example, lets her baby ride on one hip as if it is riding a pony, while the macaque mother pops her baby under her arm like a bundle of sticks. Some monkeys wear their baby dangling from a teat.

Bears, Liz was amazed to know, hold the whole head of their babies in their mouths and carry them around like a limp sack of potatoes. "I'd be scared," said Liz. "What if the mama forgets and closes her mouth?"

"Mamas don't forget," said daddy, "and the mama bear loves her baby very much. Even though it's just a baby, the little bear understands that and feels perfect trust. Animals know by instinct who loves them, who is indifferent, and who is dangerous."

One of the cutest sights, Elizabeth decided, was the way the mama elephant tries to hold hands with its baby while walking. Only since they have no hands, they touch trunks. And when the baby must follow its mother while traveling, even cuter is to see how the little one walks behind the mother, hanging onto the mother's tail with its trunk.

Naturally the silly sea otter has to do something cuter and funnier than most all the rest. The mama otter makes a little raft of seaweed, perches her baby on it, and grandly floats it around like a baby carriage, diving and showing off in front of the other otters. But probably the funniest sight is a baby hippo riding around on its big fat mama.

CHAPTER 12

I've Got Problems; the Monkey's Got Problems

You think you have problems—a youngster, perhaps, who is not bringing home the kind of grades you'd like? Well, animals too have to cope with kids who won't learn. Consider the frustration of the mother sea otter who had to stand by watching as her offspring tried to figure out how to get an abalone to let loose of a rock so he could have it for dinner.

The sea otter, as far as scientists know, is the only animal of the sea to use tools. So this is a very big deal. Now the little otter must have watched a hundred times the way its mother took a rock and rapped the abalone smartly on the side until it let go.

But this youngster couldn't get it straight. It got the stone and it located the abalone, but instead of hitting the abalone with the stone, it put its head against the abalone and pounded its own stomach.

Hilarious to us, but it must have been frustrating for the poor mother. If that silly otter doesn't catch on soon, its days of living are numbered. An otter must eat one-fourth its weight every day, and the droppings of bits of food from other otters is strictly limited, with fish competing for the floating food.

Your child hangs onto a filthy old comfort blanket and won't let go? Have pity. Even a little sea otter out in the big ocean needs a comfort blanket. It wraps itself in a little blanket of kelp, and waits for mama otter to come home.

Your child eats too much and you're worried that he or she will get fat? You're right to worry. Lots of animals who come in contact with humans develop the habit of overeating. But few develop it on their own and in the wild. It has been noticed that overweight people have overweight dogs, and that overweight people raise overweight children.

The problem is that some people insist on rewarding their children, and their pets with candies and rich foods. Also, people reward themselves with food to overcome a feeling of rejection. The best kind of reward that can be given to loved ones is praise.

Children love praise for a job well done, and a dog enjoys words of praise which sound sweet to his ear, and a pat on the head.

A well-known veterinarian, Dr. Lloyd Prasuhn, of Chicago, was concerned that humans were inflicting their own bad eating habits on their dogs, causing these poor creatures to develop man's own debilitating diseases—heart troubles, breathing difficulties, and stiff, painful joints.

The animals have enough problems of their own. They don't need ours.

The dog doesn't have our intelligence to go on diets, but what's the excuse of humans for excessive weight gain? Psychiatrists link obesity with lack of confidence.

But getting back to dumbness and smartness in the animal kingdom, the animals you see in the world are indeed the cream of the crop. The weak ones have already been weeded out through natural selection. A rabbit or fox who doesn't learn its mother's lessons well on how to take evasive action, and run a crooked course with backtracking, will fall prey to the first pack of hunter's dogs.

Sometimes a little squirrel shows its low IQ by having a very foggy memory of where it has hidden its nuts and other seeds. It may have been as industrious as the others in gathering and "squirreling" away its bounty for the winter, but when the snow flies, it doesn't mean a thing if he can't find where the little stores are hidden.

I'm trying to get the girls, young as they are, to evaluate what they see around them—what is dumb and what is smart. We are always seeing which animal could have done something another way.

But just because an animal did it, doesn't make it smart. If human animals follow the examples of a dumb animal, the family is quick to point a finger. Once, I had hidden away a sandwich I planned to eat a little later, and it was not uncovered until it had mold on it.

Liz pointed the finger. "You followed a dummy, Daddy."

"Whom did I follow?" I asked, forgetting.

"A dummy squirrel," she said. "You should have been a bear, and hidden it in your tummy, if you wanted it. Or put it in the refrigerator to share like a nice prairie dog."

"Touché," I said. "You're right."

* * *

Any couple who is constantly around each other will have things to argue about. The problem is whether or not to let the children hear parents argue. Some parents brag that their children have never heard them argue or say a cross word to each other. That is because they do it behind closed doors.

In one such case, the parents got a divorce, and their only child was terribly upset because he had not been prepared for it. He never heard them arguing. He actually felt they had gotten a divorce because of something he had said or done. Children are apt to blame themselves for not having been able to hold their parents' marriage together. But in this case, the secrecy of the parents resulted in exaggerated guilt feelings.

In another case I know of, the worried children knew there was fighting going on behind closed doors and felt that the argument had to be about them.

Being secretive causes more problems than it solves. Besides, only by hearing how their parents handle disagreements can children learn how to reason.

I agree with the psychiatrist, Arline Caldwell, of the Roosevelt Hospital in New York City, who said that happy families are those who learn how to talk out their differences.

At our house, we sit down and chatter, monkey style, until it's out of our systems. But we've added a rule that monkeys don't have. With the monkeys, everybody screams, and nobody listens.

In Monkeytown, the angry chattering goes on and on until somebody gets scared and runs away, or gets bored and walks away, or the head monkey comes over and gives them the evil eye. That quiets them. The king has made his wishes known.

Now let's visit the Cammarata household in the middle of a family argument. It's as heated as the monkey fight, but we are taking turns yelling and anyone can play, as the saying goes.

We have been doing this for years at our house.

Unless the argument is about something private, we let the little ones participate and have their say too. I call it our "egg-timer method" of clearing the air. Each person gets a three-minute turn of uninterrupted talking, while the sands are running through the egg timer.

You'd be surprised how much can be said in three minutes. The main thing is that we have a chance to get something off our chests. Each person gets as many three-minute turns as he or she needs to state a case or put up a defense. But keeping each speech down to three minutes keeps an argument from becoming a screaming match. It tends to help people talk in a logical way rather than an uncontrolled way.

Sometimes, as soon as Margy or I have understood the complaint the other one is making, we back down by saying, "I never realized it looked that way. I'll try to remember not to say that to you again."

However, sometimes we go back and forth on the three-minute turns, and one of us finally says, "We're not getting anywhere. Let's think about it and have another go at it tomorrow."

Having released some of the hostility, we might all walk down to the corner drugstore for ice cream, and not even refer to it again until the next day. And it has happened that the next day, the matter seemed very small, and a compromise was quickly reached, or one or the other has said, "Oh, it really isn't that important. If it really means that much to you, go ahead and do it."

Sometimes Liz and Michelle are interested in the subject—or just interested in being in on an adventure or the excitement of a disagreement—and they sit in on the egg-timer sessions. Other times they find it boring compared to whatever else they were doing, and they ignore it. The choice is theirs, unless they are concerned about the argument.

Sometimes the egg-timer method is used to settle a difference between the two girls, and Margy and I simply sit in on it and maybe give a three-minute opinion on either side.

The children are also permitted to give threeminute opinions in their parents' arguments. Margy and I admit freely that we are not perfect and don't always know the answers, but we want to do the best job we can. We say that this is one-way people are luckier than the animals—we can talk it over.

To which Liz once replied that the animals didn't have to talk it over because they could read each other's minds. She may be right. It is certainly true that the gift of speech has given humans the chance to be understood and misunderstood. But as long as we follow the two rules on fighting fair, the misunderstandings don't turn into something more serious.

The two rules state: Don't clam up and refuse to talk, and don't resort to name-calling or abusive language.

*   *   *

To be alive, to be a child, to have brothers and sisters with whom you must share, is to experience sibling rivalry. The experts have always maintained that a child benefits from siblings—brothers and sisters of close age—in order to learn to hold their own in this highly competitive world.

Some psychologists feel that it's a benefit to raise an only child, as there is less stress in the first few years of life when the child needs to gain confidence, more than needing to learn to compete. Let me confess that I was an only child and I turned out all right. I learned to compete in the playgrounds and had my share of bloody noses and black eyes. I think I was a more confident scrapper because felt like the king of the road because my parents made me feel important. I grew up thinking I could do anything that I put my mind to and I still believe it, within reason.

As for sharing, I learned that in being made to share special treats with my parents, and with playmates and young relatives. In fact, I probably enjoyed sharing with others more because I could afford to be gracious. I knew that the friends or relatives would eventually go home and I would again be king of the castle. Since I have a warm-hearted Italian mother who preached sharing and wanted to share whatever she had with the world, no damage was done to my psyche, and I grew up believing that everybody in the world was, in a way, my brother or sister.

I see nothing wrong with deciding to have one child. They are only doing what the panda does, and the panda mother, raising her cub to be independent and self-assured individual.

When our second child was on her way, one reason I was so eager to take paternity leave was to maintain that same one-to-one relationship with my children that my mother had with me. In a way this did take place. I spent most of my time with Elizabeth, while Margy spent most of her time with the baby. And when we were all together, we were a happy foursome.

When I was taking care of Michelle—bathing her or changing her diaper—Liz was my happy assistant. If she seemed a little jealous, we played house, she bathing her baby doll or changing its diaper, while I did the same with my real-life baby.

Parents worry too much about an older child who starts acting babyish when a second child arrives. There is nothing wrong with being babyish at age three, four, five, or even six. The older child has sustained a terrible blow to its ego, in dropping from first place to bottom of the league.

It's perfectly natural for the older child to say, "I hate Johnny" or "I hate Susan." And when Elizabeth told me, "I hate Michelle," I did not act alarmed or tell her that she should be ashamed. That would have made her hide her true feelings.

Instead, I said, "I know how you feel. You hate Michelle because she is a new baby and everyone is making a fuss about her, don't you?"

"No," said Liz shaking her head.

I tried again. "You hate Michelle because Mommy runs to her every time she cries, and Mommy plays with her all the time."

"Yes," said Elizabeth. "Mommy doesn't love me anymore."

"I know she loves you just as much as ever," I assured her, "but I know she has been pretty busy. If I get my paternity leave, I will be spending a lot of time with you, I promise, and you and Daddy will do a lot of things together that you used to do with Mommy. Would you like that?"

Her beaming face told me the answer.

That night after I got home from work and both children were fed and asleep, Margy and I had a conference. Margy agreed that there was a problem, and she said it intensified every time a friend or relative arrived with a gift for the baby.

I had a brilliant solution, which I have since found suggested in some of the reading I have been doing on child care. I suggested that we keep a small supply of dimestore and drugstore toys on hand, and every time someone brought a gift for the baby, Margy would also give a gift to Elizabeth.

This worked out very well. Elizabeth got so that she welcomed people bearing gifts for her sister because she knew it also meant a gift for her. The only trouble was, as I recall, the night that I came up with my great idea, Margy mentioned that two friends were coming the next morning to deliver gifts.

I had to dash out into the night to find a drugstore that was still open that sold toys.

"I'm sorry about that. I guess you're hoisted on your own petard," laughed my amused wife.

*   *   *

Elizabeth takes naturally to neatness, but Michelle had to be tricked into keeping her own room straightened up. I'll admit that first I used the worst psychology. I compared her unfavorably to her sister. The more I took Michelle to see her sister's room and told her how nice it was and how good Liz was, the messier Michelle got. I realized that Michelle was going to have a little pigpen in there, and I warned her of the direction she was going and showed her pictures of pigpens.

Evidently Michelle didn't mind being a little pig.

I went a step further and piled up all the things she left strewn around her room, and changed the house, in a big heap on the bedroom floor.

Liz laughed at her with a superior air. This had no effect except to make Michelle laugh too, and show off by jumping up and down on her pile of dirty clothes and toys. Soon Liz and she were both using the pile as a sort of piggy mud wallow.

So that didn't work.

Then Mother Margy tried picking up, while Michelle was made to sit in a little chair and watch. That didn't help either.

Then, in desperation, I praised Michelle highly for the one corner of her room that was neat —her desk. No matter that it was neat, Michelle never used it, preferring to lay on the floor to do her drawing and lettering.

Michelle beamed. "Oh, how nice your desk is, Michelle," I said. "It's so neat, and I like the way you have your books arranged on it, and your crayons and colored pencils all in that little vase."

I went and got Margy and showed her how neat Michelle's desk was. And when Liz came home from school, I called her into Michelle's room to show her, too.

Michelle still beamed. The next day I asked Michelle if she would like Daddy to help her make the rest of her room look as nice as her desk. Instead of agreeing, she started out of her room waving at me to come with her.

I couldn't imagine where she was going, but she went straight as an arrow to my closet and opened my door. There it was, my own shame, a pile of dirty clothes and the sports jacket I had not bothered to hang up.

This four-year-old had shown me up for the phony I was. Here I had been preaching neatness at her, while throwing my own dirty and clean clothes on the closet floor for Margy to pick up.

I confessed. I admitted Michelle was right in showing me how unfair it was for me to be messy if she had to be neat. I became a co-conspirator, saying, "Michelle, I'm so ashamed. If you help me straighten up my mess, I'll help you straighten up yours, and I'll try to be neater tomorrow. Is that a deal? You help me, and I'll help you." Gleefully Michelle and I rushed around the room, throwing underwear down the chute and at each other, and generally making a game of getting rid of everything on the closet floor.

Soon we praised ourselves brought everyone in to see our beautiful closet and room, even Grandpa Jim and Nanny Ida from upstairs.

Now Michelle and I shared high fives when we inspect each other's rooms.

The main thing I learned from my cleanup experience with Michelle is the psychology of teaching a child to be neat. I have come to a great conclusion which I've put into a little rhyme.

Behavior is caught.

It can't be taught.

*   *   *

Elizabeth gets angry when her sister breaks a special toy or a piece of her costume jewelry. Michelle, knowing this, will take something from Elizabeth only when she is not at home, telling me she will put it back before her sister returns from school.

Since I have let her play with these things, I made sure that she returns with them gently and that they are indeed put back before Elizabeth arrives home.

The problem here is deeper than Michelle's longing to play with something pretty. She has every bit as much junk jewelry, and as many toys and games as her sister. This is a matter of sibling rivalry, and a yearning by Michelle to walk in her big sister's shoes. I tell her, in effect, that I understand and sympathize. "You wish you were as big as your sister, don't you, Michelle? I know it's hard to be a little sister, but someday you will be just as big as she is. Here, I'll help you put on her necklace, and you can pretend you are a big sister, and your doll is your little sister."

Even animal siblings show rivalry. They will shove each other away and fight over the same teat when their mother is trying to feed them. Or they will chase a feather and fight over possession of it.

The main thing with human siblings is to help them express their jealousy and not make them feel they must suppress it, only to explode in some more violent manner later.

I know of several cases where the mother kept excusing an older child's fierceness in hugging a younger child, saying, "Oh, she loves her little brother so much she could hug him to death" or "She just doesn't know her own strength."

Well, she did know her own strength, and the little girl have smothered her little brother to death. I helped the mother see that she was not solving the situation by making excuses for the older child's behavior.

When an older child tries this smothering behavior, the parent must quickly pull the older child away and tell him or her firmly not permitted to hug the baby anymore. Then you can explain, in a gentler tone, that you understand how hard it is to have a baby around, and that this doesn't mean there is any difference in the amount of love you feel for both.

Then you can add something that will prove that you haven't transferred all your love to that awful little crybaby. "I have enough love spilling over from you that I can give some to your new little brother, too."

As a final show of solidarity, make the older child feel important by helping you while you do something with the little one.

* * *

I knew that we were going to have trouble with sibling rivalry when Elizabeth, who was nearly four when Michelle was born, suddenly started acting babyish, and wanting a bottle. At first, Margy and I were going to laugh Liz out of it and tell her what a big girl she was, and how we were counting on her to be grown.

We realized then that we were lucky that Liz had given us an unmistakable signal of her feelings. So, we did the opposite and fixed two bottles at a time. I really felt a little sick as I handed Elizabeth one of Michelle's baby bottles, thinking that trouble lay ahead.

To my delight, Liz soon got bored with the bottle and didn't even finish half of it. Thereafter, when Liz again asked for a bottle, we always gave it to her freely. We also made sure that we gave her a full quota of time when we played only with her, and didn't even mention her sister.

As a result, Liz got over her problem and even started taking us over to see some cute thing baby Michelle was doing. Soon she was saying, "Why don't we take the baby over to visit the neighbors?" In her mind it was now us and the baby. Victory!

* * *

One of the problems that mothers mention is their child's refusal to come home when called.

The animals of the world have such problems, too. Baby elephants like to gallop ahead of the herd and are apt to get lost. To stop this, certain female elephants are charged with the duty of keeping the little ones back where they belong.

Among other animals, the mothers keep a sharp eye on their infants, and the offspring, in tum, keep a sharp eye on their mothers. They'd better. If they get left behind, they are really deserted—for the herd does not tum back—and predators are everywhere.

The parent who simply wants his or her child to leave its playmates and come when called must also provide an incentive. It can be a positive or a negative incentive. You can say, "If you don't come home by four o'clock, you will not be permitted to go back out to play after you eat your supper." That's a negative incentive.

A positive incentive might be some reward. "If you get home by four o'clock, you'll be able to come shopping with me." Most kids like to go shopping with their mothers so they can pick out some of the brands they like and perhaps end up with an ice-cream cone. If a car ride is involved, Elizabeth and Michelle are ready on the double, and no other reward is required.

* * *

I know parents who only give full attention to their children when they are behaving in a completely obnoxious or aggressive way. The solution is to reverse your own behavior. Try ignoring them when they behave negatively so that you will not encourage them.

"Instead, reward your child with praise or a hug when he is behaving cooperatively or working independently at something or engaged in any type of behavior you consider desirable."

That's what we do at our house, ignore the negative and praise the positive, and, I assure you, it helps.

* * *

Animals steal from each other, and monkeys squabble over ownership of a banana. Penguins steal stones, which they consider precious. Children can rise above taking whatever attracts them, if you can catch them early and show them that stealing doesn't pay.

It is very important, I found, to confront the child who has taken something, as quickly as possible, and insist that he or she make restitution. I remember a child I grew up with whose mother kept making the restitution for him. The fellow, who was my age, would steal one of my toys or some other playmate's marbles and the mothers would march over to his house to complain.

The boy would always insist the object was his, that we had given it to him, or that he had bought it. His mother would say, "Well, if he took it, I am sure he didn't mean any harm. He likes it so much it would break his heart to take it away. Let me just pay you for it."

The first time Elizabeth was found playing with a little doll that was not her own, she was made to march to the playmate's home and return the doll with an apology. We did not do her talking for her.

Another time, when she broke another playmate's toy in a fit of anger, we insisted that she earn the money to buy her little friend a replacement. She had to water plants around the house at a penny a plant. It was hard going, but when she had earned the dollar, she also had learned about the adult world of earning a living and how hard it was.

Incidentally, she also learned that mishandling other people's property doesn't pay!

*   *   *

Tensions are generally resolved at our house by not getting tense and simply refusing to get excited. If you allow your children to get the better of you, you will go absolutely mad. No matter now excited the little ones get, no matter how they scream and show their frustration and anger, I try to stay cool and talk to them in a reasonable tone.

We do not punish children for opinions they have that differ from ours, only if they have committed some act that is harmful to themselves or others. Mostly, things are very serene around the house. We found that if kids are kept in a well-disciplined environment that allows for a fair degree of freedom of speech, they will not get on your nerves as much as you think.

I must confess there are moments when we could appreciate a break—we from them and, of course, the opposite is true. At such times, a little change of environment is always good.

Other parents will have to figure out how they can get a little relief. At our house, that's when the grandparents come in and use their expertise to relax the situation, and I may take Margy to a movie. I do not pretend to be a perfect father, only a dedicated one.

As for wife Margy, the worst disagreement we have concerned my decision to write this book. The time and energy that went into it disrupted the household. It was not just the writing, but the research and the checking and the double-checking of things I thought it would be fun. But it wasn't. It was work which however I learned to enjoy.

I wanted to share my findings. I felt that there was a need for fathers to get in on the exciting adventure and learn about parenting as a shared experience with animals of every stripe and description around the world.

Margy, however, heartily disagreed. She did not think it was necessary for the world to know everything we were doing. "If it turns you on, Jerry, that's okay."

I do feel I have a commitment to parents to make them aware of my experiences, to let others take a peep into our household through the window of this book. However, her argument is as justified as mine. It's just that our approaches to this are different. She is a lioness, bringing home food for her pride. I am a prairie dog, who finds something good and shrieks for everyone to come and share.

After listening to Margy and I argue about this book and whether it should be written, Liz said quite seriously, "Daddy, are you and Mommy going to get a divorce?"

"Divorce?" I said. "Whatever made you think about divorce?"

"Well, that's how Sherry's parents sounded, and they got a divorce. But now her daddy's very nice and he buys her ice cream when he sees her every Saturday."

It was certainly true that the neighborhood had its share of divorced and visiting fathers.

"No, we will never get a divorce, baby," I assured Liz, holding her close and giving Margy a meaningful look which said we'd better cool it. "Everybody has some little disagreements. You know how Grandma and Grandpa argue upstairs now and then, but then they make up and they say they didn't really mean it.

"And you know Grandma and Grandpa aren't getting a divorce."

"Yes, I know," said Liz.

"And you know how you and Michelle are always fighting. But you're not getting a divorce, are you?"

Now she was giggling. "Of course not, that's silly, Daddy."

"Well, Daddy loves Mommy, and Mommy loves Daddy, doesn't she, Margy? And we're not getting a divorce."

"Okay," said my daughter, "but if you do, will you promise something, Daddy?"

"What?"

"Will you come to see me every Saturday like Sherry's father does and take me for ice cream?"

"Get out of here."

* * *

I said a little earlier that I try to stay calm and not discipline my children unless they are doing something harmful to themselves or others. But let me quickly confess that I have not been a plaster saint and I have gotten pretty upset when the children have annoyed me for an extended period of time. Usually, then, I have the good grace to say that I got a little too excited and may have overreacted.

I remember once it was Elizabeth who was getting on my nerves racing around and around after I told her not to, and, finally, tipping over an ashtray and breaking it. I stopped, glared at her, as she stood their crying. And saying she was sorry she had broken the ashtray, I suddenly realized how foolish it was to get so upset over a cheap dimestore ashtray. She had been trying to have fun. She had meant no wrong.

I told her that I wasn't angry anymore and that I'd been upset. "You didn't mean to do it, and I got too excited. I'm sorry."

Liz smiled through her tears and said like a little angel, "That's all right, I still love you."

*　　*　　*

Liz likes to hear about the strange goings on within the various species of animals and then she will pass judgment. She thinks it's weird for water fleas to just keep dancing their lives away and never rest. I explain that they have to keep hustling to stay above the water as they feed on tiny microscopic plants on the surface.

"Well, why don't they just settle down on the water and eat all they want? Then they can fly away."

"They don't dare, Liz," I explained. "They have a problem. The moment they stop, there is a little fish ready and eager to snap them up. You see, what it amounts to is that they are sort of dancing one step from being eaten."

"Are people like that?" asked Michelle.

"No, in the people world it would be called 'dog-eat-dog.' But you were mighty close."

*　　*　　*

One of the best real-life stories I have heard, which proves that animals can indeed use their brains to solve problems, involves a chimp. This story may have come from the personal observations of one of the greatest animal researchers, Jane Goodall.

What does stand out in my mind is the vision of a chimp growing up frustrated and doomed to a life on the periphery of his group. His problem was he wanted to be leader. Nobody challenged the leader who thumped the ground loudly if any rash adolescent came near the desirable females.

As fate would have it, humans came camping nearby with all their paraphernalia. The bright young chimp watched the humans clumping and thumping around as they prepared food and did their daily chores. Suddenly, the young bright one got the connection—he grabbed three empty kerosene cans and ran around thumping them on the ground.

Such a racket did he make that even the old bull ran off in terror. In fact, all the males fled, and the inventive one suddenly found himself numero uno of the harem. He had won a battle without shooting a gun or even throwing a fist.

When the old overlord finally figured it out, it was too late. According to the rules, he had to hit the road and hope he could find a new group to join. If he stayed, he would have to hang around on the sidelines, and, as Elizabeth well knows, even the lowest animal has his pride.

CHAPTER 13

Grandma Lives at Our House

I'll tell you something great about having grandparents in the house or in the neighborhood—they are the only persons I know who can tell your little monsters about you in a way that will bridge the generation gap. What your kids are going to learn from your parents, is that you were a little monster too.

My children have found me more lovable since Grandpa told them about my first job selling soda pop in a public hall. It seems I ran up and down the aisles yelling, "Soda, Colas, Pepsi," with my fingers inside the open necks of the bottles.

I could hold eight bottles this way—four in each hand and not have to open the bottles one at a time. I was going to make a killing on my first night in business.

My first customer shot down my balloon. She took one look at me as I came running in answer to her wave and screamed, "I don't want that soda with your fingers in it." I ran and got her a fingerless Coke, while laughter followed behind me.

The laughter I could cope with. I always tried to make people laugh and was the class clown. What really hurt was realizing I had shot my night's profits with the eight bottles of sodas, I would have to discard.

I thought everyone had forgotten this, but grandparents never forget. They choose the Strangest times to tell your child, "Oh, don't pay any attention to your daddy. I remember when he tried to sell me soda pop with his fingers in the bottles."

It does tend to bring Big Daddy down to a level where any kid can handle him.

When Margy was worried about our girls' sleep habits and afraid that my animal games were making them more active at bedtime instead of quieting them down, it was my mother who told Margy and the girls what a really active baby was like—it was me!

Once she looked in the nursery to see if I was asleep, and discovered both the crib and baby me were missing. She went screaming out of the room. She thought surely I had been kidnapped and with the crib!

While she was reaching for the phone, she heard me start to cry and ran back to the bedroom. I had gotten on my hands and knees in the crib and rocked myself across the room. My kids learned that their daddy never really got started being active until bed time.

Once when Elizabeth was in serious trouble for having thrown mud on a neighbor lady, Grandma put it in perspective. She helped soothe her dignity, telling what I had done when I was a small boy.

Then she turned to Elizabeth and told her an incident that I had long forgotten, and that I had hoped would go untold to the eventual grave of my victim, a family friend I called Aunt Helen.

Aunt Helen was walking down our street, and, for some reason, I felt a great urge to throw something at her. I ran and got an egg from the refrigerator and raced after her. Unfortunately, she turned around and caught me just as I was trying to make up my mind whether or not to throw the egg which I held in my upturned arm.

Aunt Helen said, "Jerry, you wouldn't dare." It was the worst thing she could have said. I had to throw it.

It wasn't that Aunt Helen had reported on me—she hadn't. It was that my mother had witnessed the incident, and used a little psychology of her own. And she was right. I had gotten it out of my system and, having seen what raw egg looks like running down someone's arm, was content never to try anything like that again.

So it is with grandparents. They have a gentling effect on a family, and help put little things in perspective. They are also great for pointing out your good deeds that might inspire your own children.

When Grandma and Grandpa Cammarata told with pride how their son had studied guitar at the early age of ten, and started almost immediately to entertain the sick and disabled at Public Health Hospital on Staten Island every week, Elizabeth was determined to follow in Daddy's footsteps.

"But, Liz, baby, you're only eight years old and you can't play the guitar—though I am sure some of the patients must have wished I couldn't either. But what can you do to entertain the sick people?"

"I'll tell them my jokes," she said huffily.

"Oh, my, I'm sorry," I said. I had forgotten that she had fancied herself as the jokester of the Western World.

I couldn't take her to a hospital, but I found a friend with a broken leg and let her work her healing humor on him. It was a riot:

Liz: What do you put between the bread to make an astronaut sandwich?

Hobble-leg: Hot air?

Liz: No, silly, launchmeat. You know, like a launching pad?

Hobble-leg: I know, I know.

Liz: Why won't a cat eat lemon drops?

Hobble-leg: It doesn't want to get cavities?

Liz: No, No. It doesn't want to be a sourpuss.

Liz jumped in with her next one, as my friend looked at me with surprise and said, "What have we here?"

Liz: What was the best advice that the mother kangaroo gave to her baby?

Hobble-leg: Don't hop in the wrong pouch?

Liz: "No," she said. "Don't ever accept a ride with a stranger."

"I think my friend has heard enough jokes for one day," I broke in, seeing that Liz hadn't begun to run dry.

"No, no, let her carry on," protested Dick in friendly fashion.

I could see that Liz was a little hurt, but she fought to get just one more riddle in.

Liz: Did I tell you the one about the jumping rope?

Hobble-leg: No, I don't think so.

Liz: Well, skip it!

She flounced out of the room, and he burst into laughter as he realized she really had caught him off guard.

Liz came back and took a bow, as Dick and I applauded as loudly as four hands could manage.

The reason that Liz was so well able to perform that day was the confidence that she had gotten from her grandparents. Grandparents have the time and patience to listen to a child repeat something over and over, always beaming approval, always encouraging. I am sure they must know Liz's jokes by heart. Parents do this, of course, but they are apt to run off remembering some work that's waiting. But grandparents give a child complete attention, and this does wonders for a child's development.

*　　*　　*

They also are the only ones who are able to give your children a real description of what your wedding was like.

Though our wedding was memorable, I sang at my own wedding, to the surprise of my relatives. However, the engagement scene, is the one my mind returns to at unexpected moments.

I proposed at the Christmas breakfast table at Margy's home, with her parents watching. With everyone in tears—happy ones, I hope—I said all the things that were in my heart, and slipped the engagement ring on her finger.

But time marches on, and now couples say all the memorable things in wedding vows which they write for themselves.

Even some of the wedding guests these days are a little unusual. One wedding, which is appropriate to mention here, involved the presence of 'the best friend of the bride—a full-grown boa constrictor named Bea.

Because of the presence of Bea, who was quite harmless because she had been well fed before the wedding, another best friend, understandably human, refused to attend.

I don't know what I'll do if, as a result of the emphasis on animals in our house, my girls decide to have similar guests at their weddings. If they do, they will probably invite a pool full of friendly otters, and let the guests throw abalones to them as I sing "Oh Promise Me."

* * *

When friends come to our house they are Aunt or Uncle So and So to the children. Michelle wondered why everyone was an uncle or aunt, and I told her about the friendly Hopi Indians and other cultures who believe in showing respect to their elders.

So it came to pass that a new friend came by who looked a little older than our other friends. Elizabeth, out of respect, and using her own judgment as I had taught her to, greeted her with, "Hi, Grandma."

The evening was not a success.

* * *

I'm very much in favor of several generations living under the same roof. It's working well after our shakedown cruise in which we settled the rules that are right for our household. In-laws do not pop downstairs without warning. We don't pop in on them without asking if they're open for visitors.

At first, when we had our new arrangement of young folks downstairs and older folks upstairs, Elizabeth had a little problem at school. Some children made fun of her for having to live with old people. "I'm the only one who has a Bubby in the house," Elizabeth said, crying. "Nobody else does."

So we sat down for a little session of show-andtell. Out came the books that showed how the baby elephant has older lady elephants living with it and its mommy to help it grow up. And how this was so common a practice with the elephants that it's called the Auntie System.

"Don't you see how lucky this makes the baby elephant?" I told her how even before the mama elephant gives birth to her baby she seeks out a couple of older and wiser lady elephants and gets acquainted with them. Then when the baby is born, the two older ladies, who are known as "aunties," walk on each side of the baby elephant so nobody can hurt it, and they hang around and watch over it and babysit for the mommy, just like your grandmother does. She's your auntie. Tears gone, Elizabeth smiled.

That she liked.

"Who are they protecting the baby elephant from?" Liz wanted to know.

"From tigers," I said. "They're protecting it from a tiger attack."

"But we don't have any tigers in front of our house. Why do I need to walk between aunties?"

"Well," I said, "we don't have tigers, but we have cars and trucks and motorcycles. So when you walk with Mother and Grandma or with Mother and me, we keep you safe between us."

"Who else has aunties to take care of it? Does the monkey have aunties, too?"

"Oh, lots of them," I said. "At first the real mama won't let anybody else touch her baby. She just wants to enjoy it herself. But the aunties keep coming around and that pretty soon the mother let's all the aunties take turns looking after the funny little baby."

I suddenly remembered another animal who shared child care. "Mountain sheep ladies, who are called ewes, also get together to help the mama take care of the young." I went no further. My little animal lover was sound asleep.

*   *   *

The TV movie, Roots, based on the great genealogical search by Alex Haley, made the whole nation heritage-aware, and people rushed off in all directions searching for their roots. But my children, having two sets of grandparents nearby, have never had a rootless feeling. They have always known about their roots, and have relished the family stories that go way back and tell about Granny and her granny or Grandpa and his papa.

Elizabeth likes to hear my father's stories about growing up in a large family of seven brothers and three sisters, and she is very impressed with the fact that a boy from a poor family could not find a part-time job to earn any money while he was going to school. They were so poor, they had to do everything themselves.

Some people, Liz has learned from him, could not even afford to buy a secondhand lawn mower. This time period became known to Elizabeth and the rest of the world as the Great Depression.

I remember one day coming upon Grandpa explaining it all to her in her own terms. He said, "Do you know what it is like when you get hungry and there is no restaurant around. And when you want to buy a toy and you cannot get it. That was the depression."

"What did you do?" Elizabeth asked, worried.

"We made the most of every piece of cloth or bit of food that we had. We saved and worked hard."

"Oh," beamed Elizabeth, relieved.

I don't think I could have done a better job. Grandparents really know how to get ideas across to children. I know that Liz has learned a lot about life and death from her various grandparents, and because of them she is less afraid of death, more sure that we will meet some-day even when we are gone from this earth.

I remember the day that Elizabeth was crying because her mother and I were going somewhere without her. "I don't want to be alone," she wailed.

"Don't you know, dear, all people spend time alone," my mother explained consolingly. "But being alone doesn't mean you have to be lonely. You can meet all kinds of people and animals in your books. You can keep yourself company in your own mind planning what you are going to do, or how you can surprise Mommy and Daddy. You can sit and watch the world out of the window and think any-thing you want to, make up a story."

*   *   *

Psychologists often blame the troubles parents are having with their children as most children today are growing up without the gentling influence of grandparents. Children mellow and relax more when they see the continuity between generations. Parents are a little nervous and high-strung because they are fighting the battle for survival in a financially, emotionally, and physically boo-by-trapped world.

Grandparents, on the other hand, are more relaxed. When they have a little extra money, they enjoy buying little treats for their grandchildren. Grandparents are the buddies and the confidants of little ones, and the co-conspirators.

Thanks to their grandparents, my little punkins now know that nobody's an angel, even their beloved Gramps. According to his own recent confession to Liz, when my father-in-law was a kid, he and his friends would fill whiskey bottles with water and ride the Staten Island ferry pretending that they were drunk.

Such were their simple pleasures.

Elizabeth liked this story very much and was determined to fool me. Margy's father was drawn into Liz's conspiracy. When next my wife made me bacon and eggs, Elizabeth put a plastic egg on my dish that really looked so much like the real thing that I started to eat it. Liz thought that this was very funny. Everyone was laughing and snickering at my expense.

"You see, darling," said Margy, "if you had gone to a normal office by now like all other men, our little monsters wouldn't be able to play tricks on you."

"It's all right," I said, "I'll take my chances with the little monsters." And that night I made sure I was right there when Liz squealed with fear and then delight when she got into bed and felt not an egg but a fake frog.

* * *

When my father-in-law was a little boy, his father worked nights and would come home at midnight. He wouldn't let his wife get up to cook for him. He would cook for himself. My father-in-law used to sleep in the kitchen of his tenement apartment in Chinatown, New York City. He would get up when his father came home from work and eat pork chops with vinegar and peppers with his dad— Italian soul food.

Elizabeth and I get up during the night to eat together. I didn't like to bother my wife, so I prepared the snack menu of Oreos and milk, peanut butter on crackers, or jelly and bread. I let my wife sleep in peace.

Even though I am an Italian father with all the family togetherness that this implies I do not believe a wife has to be always ready to keep her husband company at all times. It's a good example for daughters to know that their mother has her rights and a separate life, even though she does not have an outside career.

Margy has her nights out. I always take her schedule into account when making my own plans.

* * *

Michelle and Elizabeth listen to politics heatedly argued in our house almost any time we get together with the in-laws. Every viewpoint is represented; every candidate is the favorite of some father-in-law, uncle, or cousin. When Carter and Ford were met on the great political battlefield, I heard seven-year-old Elizabeth telling a friend, "Here's a picture of Jimmy Carter and here's a picture of President Ford. My daddy says one of them is going to ruin the country if he's elected and the other one is going to save the country. I wish I could vote to save the country."

"Which one is going to save the country?" piped up her friend.

"That's the only part I don't know," said Elizabeth, "but it's one of them."

When Carter won, Elizabeth was delighted to have a little girl named Amy in the White House, and set about sending her favorite riddles. She also sent some favorite animal facts courtesy of the Wrigley's gum people, the funny papers, the Pink Panther show on TV, and Sesame Street.

Anyway, as I recall, Amy Carter received such riddles as these:

Q: Dear Amy, what house is easy to carry? I'll give you a clue; it isn't the White House.
A: It's a lighthouse.

Q: Why do people put wheels on their rocking chairs?

A: So they can rock and roll.

And, finally, this one that simply knocked Liz out with the cleverness of it.

Q: Dear Amy, what would you do if you wanted to catch a squirrel?

A: You'd climb a tree and make a noise like a nut.

Years later, President Carter appointment me to be a member to the White House Conference on Families. Working with parents from around the country and particularly with the late Coretta Scott King, I began to feel a deep sense of urgency to make the family the center of all we do. I think our final report to President Carter reflected that position. Liz and Michelle were given a treat of a lifetime during our final night stay in Washington DC. With had an invitation from the White House to a reception with Amy Carter. A moment which the girls will always remember.

*   *   *

Elizabeth was very proud that in our house everyone younger is supposed to help Grandma and Grandpa upstairs. It's the rule, and one day I heard her bragging about how much help she and her daddy were to the old folks.

It was time for a talk. Out came the books, and Elizabeth learned that humans are not the only creatures in the world to help their elders. Certain birds such as the Florida scrub jay actually help their parents raise the younger birds. They do not go off to raise families of their own until their parents do not need them any longer.

The young scrub jays even act as guardians and lookouts while the parents are feeding the young, watching for snakes and other predators.

One of the best examples of the young helping the older members of the family takes place among the dolphins. If an older dolphin is injured or disabled, the young and the old rush to its aid, lifting it up with their own bodies so that it can get air above the water, as needed. Such help is freely given, and nothing is expected in return. More and more, I think, man is coming to find out that not all animals are selfish, just as not all people are selfish or unselfish. There's a great variety.

* * *

As I write this book, Michelle is four and full of dignity. I think what is good about grandmothers and grandfathers is that they have lived long enough to know about such things, and treat their grandchildren with great dignity. Unfortunately, parents do not always.

Michelle's nose was out of joint. Her mother had laughed at her in front of her sister's little friend. No matter that it was a minor incident, she had been robbed of her dignity.

I told a story so she would not feel so alone. A friend's curly haired poodle had to be shaved because of a skin disorder. When we saw him looking quite naked, we all began to laugh. So insulted was the poodle, he hid for a week until his hair started to grow again, along with his dignity.

* * *

Not having to worry about survival and about getting a husband off to work every morning, grandmothers have time for many delightful projects with children. My mother liked to make toys for Michelle and Elizabeth, using the most unbelievable combination of odds and ends. In fact, they played a game in which she challenges them to find bits of scrap cloth, metal, wood, buttons-what have you.

The children were fascinated with everything she made—with their help, of course. But the magic that amazed me most was when she made animals from strips of wool and coat hangers. The children's rooms were enriched with the imaginative creatures created by a woman who loved them very much. They proudly showed her handiwork to their friends-adding, of course, that they helped make them.

* * *

Elizabeth is at a stage where she is worried that she will eventually grow up and have to leave home, so she is checking up on the life patterns of the animals. She likes the idea of the wild goose that grows up and flies south with its parents and other geese in communal living. But her favorite is the elephant calf because it stays with the mother the longest time in an extended babyhood of about seven or eight years.

We do a lot of talking at our house about how the conditions of a child's life these days has improved, as compared with days gone by. But there still is a way to go to help small children feel a part of our adult world.

I think that grandparents are the greatest crime stoppers we have going for us today. If parents cannot show enough love, who better than grandparents, do care?

*   *   *

Our government must make a concerted effort to help families. I am more convinced than ever that paternity leave is one very important the answer to solving the issues around families today. And paternity leave should not just be when a child is born, but sporadically during the early impressionable years.

Right now, every father-to-be in the United States who works for a company that offers a maternity leave can immediately apply for and receive a paternity leave equal to the maternity leave clause. If the employer refuses the request, the employee can petition the Federal Equal Employment Opportunities Commission.

But first, for fathers who seriously desire a paternity leave, they need to become aware of the beneficial effect that it can have on their families. Big business, in turn, needs to be receptive to the family-unit crisis in America today and become involved in doing more for the families of their employees. Monetary programs also need to be established to help parents during the time spent on leave.

*   *   *

My friends think I'm a little weird to be so concerned about the family.

And what does Dr. Margaret Meade, the famed anthropologist, recommend? Exactly what I have been advocating all along, and have been practicing in our home. Speaking of the ideal communities of the future, she believes we should build communities where the future of the family will be safe, with parents, aunties and uncles, and with the concept of families remaining strong among generations.

Just as with the animal kingdom, we all benefit and are shaped by the lone, time spent and attention that we receive from those close to us. The wild kingdom at our home is being rewritten everyday by the evolving family.

Epilogue

What an adventure life can be if you open yourself up to pursuing every opportunity you know instinctively. You will serve your family well. When I decided to try for a paternity leave to help raise my daughter, I did not realize then that I was starting down a road of not only expanding my own horizon, but helping others to expand theirs.

Eventually, I was appointed as the Staten Island member of the New York City Central Board of Education and, concurrently appointed Commissioner of The Department of Youth and Community Development by Mayor Giuliani. Today, I am the Chief Operating Officer, Dean of Student Affairs and Associate Professor at Touro College of Osteopathic Medicine in New York.

Along the way I had some fun too; I firmly believe avocations are an essential part of the human experience. I was a musician, and actively supported music in all its forms. During my learning days at New Dorp High School, I did summer stock theatre at Ephrata Star Playhouse in Pennsylvania. With my Actor's Equity and Screen Actors Guild cards in hand, I enjoyed acting in some really great productions. Fun is important; never let it out of your life. Keep things in balance. The fun you have will be reflected in the fun you can create for your own family.

But my proudest achievement has been my lifelong advocacy for families and Paid Family Leave. Times have changed since I first wrote, *The Fun Book of Fatherhood*. Parents today "get it" – more so than my generation did. They increasingly see raising children as an involved parent solution, and they purposefully adjust their lives accordingly. I take some small measure of satisfaction in that.

Today, we have a better understanding of how the animal kingdom serves us to help raise our children, upon which I so richly relied to write this book. It is a more acceptable strategy now, noting nothing worthwhile actually goes out of style – it just depends on how you use it.

My family prospered, and is rich in love and respect for our community. My oldest child, Elizabeth, is with the City University of New York. My middle daughter, Michelle, is an osteopathic primary care physician. My youngest, Jerry, is a CPA. And, with the mother of our children, Margaret, well, I think we did a pretty good job of helping the next generation feel responsible for the way the world turns.

I will never forget the basic principles of parenting given to us by the Eunice Kennedy Shriver National Institute of Child Health and Human Development:

- Respond to your child in an appropriate manner.
- Prevent risky behavior or problems before they arise.
- Monitor your child's contact with his/her surrounding world.
- Monitor your child to support and encourage desired behaviors.
- Model your own behavior to provide a consistent, and positive example to your child.

Ending *The Fun Book Of Fatherhood* is like having already opened the presents under the Christmas tree. Can there be much more? Well, I have experienced a great and rewarding life thus far, and witnessed three wonderful children come of age to find success – each in their own way. But completing this book is not my ending – and hopefully not the ending for you, the reader.

We must stand up and be counted – and be counted again. This epilogue is the battle cry. Let's be certain the next generation gets an equal playing field with all kinds of moms and dads sharing parenting in as many ways as they see fit, not as our corporations dictate.

As parents, we have the responsibility to keep our children safe and healthy, to educate and prepare our children to be the energized citizens of tomorrow, and to inculcate them with our precious values (as varied as they are in our beautifully mosaic society). If you can do this, you get a gold star from the American Psychological Association for having a 'high quality' parent-child relationship.

Wherever you can be influential—at work, in politics, at your church or synagogue or mosque—raise your voice on behalf of parents who need every bit of support to do their job even better.

We should not have to wait generations for a national policy from Congress, or a global policy from the U.N., recognizing that PAID PARENTING LEAVE is in the best interest of families, communities, businesses and society at large. We know it is! A Paid Family Leave national policy *MUST* be put into place now in the United States. So many other countries currently offer it. Let your voice be heard – let your vote be counted. Make family the supporting pillar of our great country. Do not depend on corporations to make decisions on how much time parents will get to spend with their children. Happy growing families with loving parents around, will truly help make our companies more successful.

Before our eyes the global impact of not having a universal family leave plan across all our international borders is causing not only family stress, but may become an epidemic which will infuse decay in our global economies. For example, the birth rate in Norway, where generous maternity and paternity leaves are given, is suffering as a result of an economic downturn. This in turn, is redefining the birth rate of the country which is compounding the economic crisis. The lesson to be learned is that just giving generous family leaves is not the answer. The answer lies in the confluence of economic strategies plus family support services creating a social and economic basis for families to grow and thrive. Norway is the example of how interwoven public policies must be in order for generous family leaves to be effective and therefore contribute to a country's overall growth.

Echoing this dilemma, the United States in the early 21st Century is doing nothing more than calling for a paid 6-week family leave policy, while concurrently calling for a cut to social service programs – the very programs which must be available to these parents for assistance. Clearly, when government fails to manage the needs of its families in a comprehensive and reflective manner, the "haves" get by and the "have nots" succumb. The United States gives only 7% of working parents any kind of paid parental leave. Ask yourself this question: should a white collar worker at Starbucks get better paid family leave than the barista? Actually, Starbuck's gives three times a better family leave benefit to its white collar workers than its baristas. Embarrassing.

The essence of family should not be defined in 'class' terms, rather through a universal expression of dignity and support. Class distribution in the manner in which we take care of our families in America today will be a tumor of uncontrollable growth, destroying our families, and thus, our country, as we want it to be one hundred, two hundred and a millennium into the future.

I suggest that our young parents today follow in the mantra of Facebook's Mark Zuckerberg. At a recent commencement address at Harvard University, he rallied the graduating class of 2017 to go forth with a purpose. Not just a purpose to be successful, but to have a purpose in life to make society better – nationally and globally. I applaud those young parents of today who are stepping up to the plate and are conducting their life with purpose – giving back to society so to speak.

LET US NOT FORGET THE STRUGGLES OF EQUAL RIGHTS THROUGHOUT HISTORY, BUT PARTICULARLY RELATING TO PARENTING. THE 20TH CENTURY SECOND WAVE FEMINIST MOVEMENT, THROUGH THE WORK OF BETTY FRIEDAN, GLORIA STEINEM, MURIEL FOX, AND DR. ELEANOR PAM, AND MANY OTHERS, CREATED THE PLATFORM WHICH IT TURNED OUT ALSO ENCOURAGED DADS TO PROCLAIM THEIR RIGHTS TO BE ALL THEY COULD BE – IN THE HOME AND AS A PARENT.

My purpose for the last forty years has been to put the family first in our pursuit of work and a valued economy, and to wake up the lethargic body of political stake holders to work towards the day when our national and global society honors the family and pronounces family leave as a right.

Do share this book with young parents, and give them an opportunity to contemplate their responsibilities to the future survival and welfare of the family, and to explore new ways to raise their kids. After all, this book is filled with imagination and practical ways of enjoying children. As the animals have raised their young, each of us as parents can do it OUR WAY! But, you need time to plan your parenting, and time to practice it. Moms and dads need time to enjoy their shared parenting. And, single parents, need the same opportunity to be the best parent he or she can and wants to be. PAID FAMILY LEAVE LEVELS THE PLAYING FIELD, AND PUTS THE NEWLY FRAMED FAMILY OF THE 21ST CENTURY FRONT AND CENTER WHERE IT BELONGS.

As for me, I am hard at work writing – more about the future of the family than of the past. What have we learned? What goals still must be achieved? Can there be a better plan that leads us to a more satisfying family life? How will technology, medical science and world economics impact what we believe is best for our families? Will the 21st Century be defined by clever talk, or by global policies supporting the rise of the family?

What does the President of the United States with congress need to do to pass national legislation to make Paid Family Leave available to all now—whether you live in New York, Utah or Wyoming, or work for Ford Motors, for a mining company, for a small business or in Silicon Valley —EVERY PARENT MUST BE SUPPORTED, CELEBRATED AND ENCOURAGED TO RAISE MAGNIFICENT CHILDREN, WHO WILL BECOME THE NEW FABRIC OF THESE UNITED STATES.

The battle cry is *FAMILY FAST FORWARD* – and you will hear this over and over again until parents and kids win – I promise you!

PARENTING LETTERS

The Spotlight is On You, Dear Super Pop

During the writing of the original book, *The Fun Book of Fatherhood*, and then throughout the years leading up to this revised edition of *The Fun Book of Fatherhood*, I have been a "Super Pop" of sorts. Parents and children have communicated their problems, concerns and even their solutions. Well, I took their comments very seriously over the years and tried to answer as many of the letters as I could, as clearly as I could, and, often, having to be as blunt as I was.

Some of the letters I received were addressed to "Dear Jerry" and some to "Dear Mr. C." But the salutation that I admit I most enjoyed was "Dear Super Pop."

I am currently compiling *Parenting Letters,* a question and answer book about raising children, using the words from parents and even children. What is always clear in my mind, however, is there are many ways to resolve an issue. I try to have parents and children understand that I may give advice, but it is just that—advice.

And, so, the adage applies: Answers to parenting are as multiple as there are parents.

Let us all marvel as to how well we did as children and how well we are doing as parents.

I would enjoy receiving your comments on parenting—your issues, your solutions and even how good your remedies were. Your words of wisdom may be an important part of a chapter in *Parenting Letters.* Please feel free to write:

Dr.jerrycammarata@gmail.com

TEACHING MOMENTS USING THE ANIMALS

A guide to your examples at home with your children

Chapter 1 – THE ANIMALS OF THE ZOO ARE ALIVE AND WELL

- Snuggling with Kids and Nurturing – Kangaroo
- Fatherhood – Not like the Phalarope
- Parental sharing of responsibilities – Couvade, Penguins
- Playing Too Hard – Lions, Beavers, Otters, Bats
- Conformity/Selfishness – Chickens

Chapter 2 –DADDY'S HOME

- Extended Family – Sheep, Elephants,
- Good Daddies/Not So Good Daddies – Coyotes/Hyenas

Chapter 3 – THE ORANGUTAN DID IT FIRST

- Newborn feats – Porcupines, Crocodiles, Alligators, Mice, Monkeys, Baboons, Orangutans Chimpanzees, Gorillas, Koala Bears
- Weaning Babies – Walruses, Elephants
- Seeing Colors – Fish, Bulls
- Toileting – Rats, birds, Honeybees
- Recognizing Mama – Orangutans
- Running – Duck Hawks, Cheetahs

- Birth Weight – Blue Whales
- Caring for Parents – Termites, Wild Dogs

Chapter 4 – FEEDING TIME AT OUR ZOO

- Feeding – Moles
- Eating Etiquette – Lizards, Anteaters, Giraffe, Snakes, Elephants, Horseshoe Crabs,
- Overeating – Dogs and Cats
- Meat Eaters – Lions, Tigers
- Vegetarians – Antelope, Gorillas, Horses
- Eating the right Food – Birds, Otters, Lions
- Rules of the Table when eating – Giraffes, Monkeys, Otters, Raccoons, Cats

Chapter 5 – DON'T MONKEY AROUND WITH A KANGAROO

- Protection – Kangaroos, Deer, Cheetahs
- Animals Talk – Beavers, Snakes, Birds, Dogs, Skunks, Swallowtail Caterpillars, Zebras,   Vicunas
- Fearfulness – Octopus, Kangaroos, Fish, Skunks, Mink, Shrew, Musk Oxen, Horses
- Camouflage – Chameleon

Chapter 6 – THANKFULLY I'M NOT A SEA HORSE

- Being Born – Chicken and Ostrich Eggs, Birds and the Bees
- Appearances – Turtles, Monkeys
- Sex Organs – Walrus, Whale, Barnacle, Turtle
- Mating – Barnacle, Clamworm, Rabbits, Pandas, Chimpanzees, Spiders, Porcupines, Otters, Goby Fish, Damsel Fly, Praying Mantises, Elephants, Shrimp, Aphids
- Eggs – Whale, Codfish. Seahorse, Sticklebacks, Water Bugs, Penguins
- Sex Changes – Limpet, Oysters, Starfish, Worms, Hagfish
- Hiding Food – Chipmunk

Chapter 7 – EVEN A FISH GOES TO SCHOOL

- Going to School – Geophagus Scymnophilus Fish, Beavers
- Seeing Color – Birds, Bulls, Primates, Fish, Bees, Butterflies
- Dominance – Bull Gorillas
- Natural Disaster/Rain – Wasps, Beavers, Termites, Robins, Ants
- Smart & Dumb – Penguins

Chapter 8 – THE GAMES ANIMALS PLAY

- Playfulness – Otters, Cats, Domestic and Wild Cats, Red-Throated Loons, Dolphins, Whales, Lions
- All Work – Termites, Bees, Ants
- Kids winning – Lion Cubs,
- Animal Games – Wild Ducks, Birds, Adelie Penguins, Owls, Kittens & Puppies, Badgers, Lions, Tigers, Blue Tit Birds,
- Weird Q&A – Rhinoceros, Elephants, Hummingbirds, Echidnas

Chapter 9 – SLEEPING AROUND

- No Home – Gorillas, Gibbons, Monkeys, Penguins. Hermit Crab, Frogs
- House Building – Ants, Oriole, Lyre Birds
- Sleep Time – Bears, Elephants, Owls
- Night Sleep – Wolves, Owls
- Sleeping Positons – Bears, Elephants, Wild Dogs
- Imitation – Bowerbirds,
- Households – Birds, Elephants, Armadillos, Rabbits,
- Territory – Wild Horses, Vicunas, Dogs, Birds, Hyenas, Badgers

Chapter 10 – ARE ALL CREATURES PART OF A GREATER PLAN

- Search for Food – Gallflies, Water Shrews, Armadillos
- Animal Helpers – Birds, Shrimp,

- Immortality – Salmon, Golden Plover Fly
- Attractiveness – Turtle, Birds, Fish, African Lion, Otters, Beavers, Monkeys

Chapter 11 – WHAT KIND OF PARENT ARE YOU

- Good Mom – Rabbits, Octopus, Salamanders, Lemur Monkeys, Hyenas, Birds, Ducks, Whales, Kangaroos, Gibbons, Bears, Elephants,
- Good Mom and dad – Gulls
- Tough Moms – Waterfowl
- Super Pops – Emus, Ostriches, Wild dogs
- Henpecked – Toads,
- Dad be gone – Beavers
- Timid Dad – Lions, Sea Otters; Larks
- Parentless – Fish, Oysters
- It's My Baby – Bears, Goats,
- Dumb Parenting, Monkeys, Penguins, Chickens

Chapter 12 – I'VE GOT PROBLEMS, THE MONKEY'S GOT PROBLEMS

- Using Tools – Sea Otters,
- Forgetfulness – Baby Rabbits, Squirrels, Foxes,
- Running Astray – Baby Elephants

Chapter 13 – GRANDMA LIVES AT OUR HOUSE

- The calming effect grandparents have
- The wisdom of grandparents
- The patience of grandparents
- The respect of addressing elders
- Mountain sheep and Elephants are great aunties.

I encourage you to send this letter to the President of the United States and your Congress Person:

Date:

Dear President or Honorable _____ (www.usa.gov/ elected-officials)

Parents across our United States today continue to find it more and more difficult to spend quality time with their children because it requires the parents to work more and more hours, with less and less required quality of time in the home, neglecting participation in early development skills and nurturing. Some companies offer paid family leave but the vast majority of our companies do not. The children of our great country should not be divided into the lucky few and the suffering many.

(You can add a family experience of your own here if you desire)

It is time my government speaks to its parents and to the next generation of its citizens and passes a law guaranteeing paid family leave to all. Young parents need this and deserve this. Older parents need this and deserve this to take care of their aging parents. There is a cooperative decision which can be reached by our government, corporate America and our parents when it comes to sharing the cost for such a valuable national pro-family policy.

President/Congressperson/Senator.................., don't delay getting involved. Parents cannot wait until tomorrow. Children do not grow up tomorrow. The time is now, the future strength of our country depends upon enlightened families with involved parents. Your work can help this matter by passing Paid Family Leave legislation now.

I await your action and a national bill on Paid Family Leave which can make the families of these great United States very proud.

Sincerely,
Name
Address
Phone
Email Address

The Nicotra Family – Michelle, Julia,
Joe, Anna, and there dog Jack.

The Cammarata Family – Alessandra, Jerry, Marisa, and Anthony

What Have They Said About The Fun Book Of Fatherhood

"Jerry became the beacon of hope for dads throughout the country, if not the word because of his historic decision to put his family first. His journey down the path of parenting and being granted the first paternity leave will have a lasting effect on future national and global policies. Granting Jerry a paternity leave was one of the most profound decisions made by me and unanimously by members of the New York City Central Board of Education. Reading his Fun Book about how he raised his children, well, it was a treasured experience."

Steve Aiello, Past President of the
New York City Board of Education.

"A story well told, with humor and sensitivity by the father awarded the first paternity leave from the New York City Board of Education 45 years ago."

Dr. Hazel Dukes – Past National President
and Board Member, NAACP

"Jerry's story provides reassurance by both Moms and Dads, especially in today's online world, that rule books and how-to-guides are not needed for parents or children, and that the greatest joy of parenting is making it up as you go along."

Ron Kuby, Civil Rights Lawyer &
former Radio Talk Show Host.

"Government needs to listen to what Dr. Cammarata is saying about being able to enjoy parenting. Government and business must see the family as the center of our culture which will be the future success of our nation. Working toward a national family leave policy is another moment in our civil rights journey. Jerry gets it."

David Paterson, Former Governor of New York.

"What a marvelous story about finding human parenting skills through observing the animal kingdom, and to better understand how best to live on this planet. Every parent should read this book."

Marilyn Vasta,
Climate Activist and Psychotherapist

"Jerry Cammarata has again written one of the most essential books for parents and their children."

Stan Corwin, Author of THE CREATIVE
WRITER'S COMPANION.